Unknown Facets of Rajiv Gandhi Jyoti Basu Indrajit Gupta

Attention Authors

'We Convert Fighters into Writers'. That's the motto of Manas Publications since more than four decades. Our message to the world is that India can win the battle not only by the bullet but also by the pen. There is no dearth of intellectuals in our country, but their knowledge is confined to them only. No sincere effort has been made by any other publisher to channelise their knowledge in national interest. That is why the talent of a large number of intellectuals remains latent. An author transforms his knowledge into a manuscript, and it is our job to spread his/her knowledge by converting it into a beautiful book. For over four decades, Manas has been motivating the intellectuals by publishing their manuscripts and would like to publish your manuscript too. So if you or your colleagues have any manuscript ready for publication or are working on it, kindly contact us with detailed synopsis and list of contents. We will transform your work into a valuable publication. If you wish, we can also suggest you the suitable subjects for writing the books related to your area of expertise. Manas is known for its publishing quality and commitments. We take utmost care in production and give wide publicity to the book as well as its author through our national and international distribution network.

Unknown Facets of Rajiv Gandhi Jyoti Basu Indrajit Gupta

Dr AP Mukherjee, IPS (Retd.)

Former

Director : CBI
Governor : Mizoram
DGP : West Bengal
Spl Secretary : M/o Home Affairs
Advisor : Union Home Minister
Member : Administrative Reforms Commission

Manas Publications
(We Convert Fighters into Writers)
New Delhi-110002 (INDIA)

MANAS PUBLICATIONS
(We Convert Fighters into Writers)
(Publishers, Library Suppliers, Importers & Exporters)
4402/5-A, Ansari Road (Opp. HDFC Bank)
Darya Ganj, New Delhi-110 002 (India)
Off. ✆ 23260783, 23265523, Fax: 011-23272766
E-mail: manaspublications@gmail.com
manaspublications@yahoo.com

ISBN 978-81-7049-470-6
₹ 595/

Designed at
Manas Publications

Printed in India at
RK Offsets Press, Delhi
and Published by Mrs Suman Lata for
Manas Publications, 4402/5-A, Ansari Road
(Opp HDFC Bank),
Darya Ganj, New Delhi-110 002 (INDIA)

Contents

Preface

This book on Jyoti Basu, Rajiv Gandhi and Indrajit Gupta, is quite unusual as it not only fills the void in our existing literature on our politics and administration of the immediate past but also has deep implications for India's current politico-administrative milieu.

How I wish we had in our midst the suave and able administrator like Jyoti Basu, an equally suave and modern man like Rajiv Gandhi, and the tough and straight-talking Indrajit Gupta. A combination like the above would have been too good to be true in the current political and administrative atmosphere!

My narrative starts chronologically with Jyoti Basu, who was the longest serving chief minister of West Bengal. My association with him dates back to 1967-68 during the violent upsurge of CPM, later know as the Naxalbari movement.

This was the first Naxal upsurge in India which erupted in the Naxalbari region of Darjeeling District covering Naxalbari, Khoribari and Phansidewa police stations of Siliguri sub-divisions. During that period, I havppened to be the Superintendent of Police of the District.

The Naxal movement came into existence at the time of the formation of the first United Front (UF) government, with Ajoy Mukherjee of Bangla Congress as the Chief Minister and Jyoti Basu as Deputy. As subsequent narratives would show, I was summoned by the Chief Minister and the Deputy CM on some occasions, which provided me my first exposure to the highest levels of the state government. On one such occasion, the CM Ajoy Mukherjee virtually goaded me into liquidating as many Naxals (then knows as CPM extremists) as we could since he was there to back us up!

Fortunately, Jyoti Basu was present in that meeting and could restrain the recklessness of the CM. Even after becoming the Chief Minister, and that too for a record number of years, he showed commendable restraint and balance of judgement, at times even defying the wishes of his party stalwarts.

By the time Rajiv Gandhi become India's Prime Minister after the gruesome assasination of his mother Indira Gandhi, Subash Ghising of the Darjeeling Gorkha Hill Council (DGHC) had unleashed a regin of terror in the hill district of Darjeeling. We, in the Kolkatta Police Special Branch, had credible intelligence that Ghising was being goaded into such reckless violence by some of the officers of one or two intelligence agencies of the Government of India, primarily with the objective of weakening the hold of the CPM in Darjeeling district, especially in its Siliguri sub-division. Some people in Delhi took this bait, without realizing that this was an extremely hazardous and short-sighted step which was bound to be counter-productive in the long run. Fortunately, the then Prime Minister, Rajiv

Gandhi, too realized the above and took steps to de-escalate Ghising-led violence. This was made possible during the Rajiv Gandhi-Jyoti Basu-Ghising meeting at Darjeeling Raj Bhavan where I too was present as the initiator of the above process. In due course, Rajiv Gandhi also appreciated our efforts in this regard.

When in late 1996, I received an unexpected telephone call from the formidable Member of Parliament, Shri Indrajit Gupta, I was literally taken by surprise. I had never met him before, when he 'humbly' requested me to brief him on the Union Home Ministry where he was about to be sworn in as the Home Minister, within the next couple of days. Thus began another chapter in my life as Advisor to the Union Home Minister.

All the above developments have been duly mentioned by me in some detail in the three chapters devoted to Jyoti Basu, Rajiv Gandhi and Indrajit Gupta, respectively. In the final and concluding chapter, I have attempted a brief overview of corruption which has assumed an extremely disturbing character, overlapping virtually all spheres of our national life.

AP Mukherjee, IPS (Retd)

Chapter 1

Jyoti Basu

Let me begin with Jyoti Basu because, chronologically, my association to him dates back to 1967-68 during the violent movement of CPM extremists later known as the Naxalbari movement. This was the first Naxalite upsurge in India, which erupted in the Naxalbari region (covering Naxalbari, Khoribari and Phansidewa police stations of Siliguri sub-division) of Darjeeling district when I happened to be its Superintendent of Police (SP), perhaps the youngest in the State then. The Naxalite upsurge erupted in the open on 3rd March, 1967, hardly a day after the formation of the first United Front government in West Bengal with about 14 disparate political parties, with Ajoy Mukherjee of Bangla Congress as the Chief Minister and Jyoti Basu of the CPI(M) as the Deputy Chief Minister.

I need not go into details about the formation of the first UF government in West Bengal, the first multi-party coalition government not only in West Bengal but perhaps in India as well. As subsequent narratives would show, I was summoned by the Chief Minister and the Deputy Chief Minister on some occasions, which provided my first exposure to the highest levels of the government. On one such occasion, when I was the SP of Darjeeling district, I was asked by the formidable Inspector General of Police Upananda Mukherji, JP, IP1 to meet him in his chamber in the Writers' Buildings (the West Bengal government secretariat as also the WB Police headquarters) because the Chief Minister wanted to talk to me regarding the Naxalbari situation. Accordingly, I had to come down to Calcutta from Darjeeling district, called on the IGP as desired, without the slightest inkling as to why the Chief Minister wanted me to meet him. The IGP did not enlighten me as to why I was thus summoned by the CM. He just asked me to accompany him to the Chief Minister's chamber.

How many guns do you have

What followed next was something for which I was totally unprepared nor did it appear that the IGP himself was fully privy to what the Chief Minister wanted me to do. After some preliminary queries about the prevailing situation in the Naxalbari region, the Chief Minister abruptly asked me about the number of guns which we then had in the Darjeeling District Police. Honestly speaking, I did not readily have with me the exact number of our firearms but could only give an approximate number, which was a little more than three hundred rifles/muskets and some carbines. What the Gandhian Chief Minister told me thereafter, was something which took me completely by surprise: '*Tobey aar ki, Communist Betaader Siksha Dewaar Jonney to Eguloi Jathesta...*'. [So, what is the problem! These many guns should be good enough to teach a lesson to the Communist rascals...']. Perhaps the IGP Upananda Mukherji himself had not anticipated this kind of outburst by the Chief Minister, and the IGP also could surmise that my response was not going to be very palatable to Ajoy Babu. Hence, he quickly intervened and told the Chief Minister that he would again have more detailed discussions with the SP and see how best and how quickly the situation could be dealt with. Having said this, the IGP stood up and asked me to accompany him to his chamber, which I did.

But I was still not reconciled to the fact that the Chief Minister would summon me just to tell that I was to use as much force as possible, including the use of guns which we then had in the district, to teach the Communists a lesson, irrespective of the casualties and other consequences, because the Chief Minister was there to back us up! It was plainly a bizarre experience for me that a well-known Gandhian for decades could make such utterances, plainly goading the police into senseless, reckless 'armed police' operations. Obviously, I did not bite the bait and for good reasons, as can be seen from my document-based account of the Naxalite movement of the period titled the Maoist Spring Thunder: The Naxalite Movement (1967-72)[2].

I had occasion to explain to Upananda Mukherji a couple of times earlier, as I did this time again in his chamber, about the overall strategy which I proposed to follow in dealing with this new kind of left extremist movement and the rationale behind the same. The IGP's antipathy, as also of a few other senior officers both in IAS and IPS to the Communists, was a public knowledge. But I must admit that the IGP was generous enough to give a long rope to this young SP's contrary viewpoints and allowed me to try out, as he conceded, a 'new approach' though not in conformity with his own views!

Nearly, three years later in 1969 on the eve of his retirement, I was privileged to receive from Upananda Mukherji a handwritten note in which he was ungrudging in his appreciation of the strategy which I had chalked out and followed up during those troubled days. The Note, among other things read thus:

> ... *The strategy which you formulated during the Naxalbari disturbances is something unique in the history of police operations in our country. Your strategy needs wide publicity and it should be borne in mind by every police officer faced with similar crisis. In view of the recent developments, there might be need for such a strategy in near future in our country. Your strategy to take the local people into fullest confidence is also a great lesson.... The failure of the departments to solve the problem of distribution of land to landless labourers has been rightly pointed out by you. The germ of future unrest is not killed. It will spread the disease in future wherever it will find a scope. Your enunciation of the West Bengal Land Reforms Act is very correct...*[3]

Facing the Cabinet over "Operation Crossbow"

I was in for many more shocks and exposures to the style of functioning of the government at the highest level and that too of a disparate coalition government to boot. Perhaps it was for the first time that the SP of a district, and that too the youngest SP in the state then, was again summoned in July, 1967 to appear before the full cabinet meeting to defend his operational plans to deal with the increasing left extremist violence of a new kind. Code named "Operation Crossbow" this was drawn up by me after detailed discussions with a high-powered Cabinet Committee[4] which visited Siliguri on 12-17 June, 1967 to study the situation on the ground and to issue necessary directions to the local administration to deal with the emerging developments.

Irrespective of their portfolios, the Committee was authorised by the Cabinet to issue advice and directions to the local authorities as may be called for. In view of their understandable initial hesitation in accepting the veracity of our reports, the ministers held separate discussions with their local party leaders and also visited some of the critical village areas individually, unaccompanied by anyone from the local administration.

In our meeting with the Cabinet Committee on 14 June, 1967, all its members came round to the view that police operations of certain magnitude against the extremists could not be avoided. So I was asked to draw up detailed plan(s) of operation which may be discussed and approved by them, a copy of which they wanted to carry with them to Calcutta for the information of their cabinet colleagues, besides the Chief Minister and the Deputy Chief Minister.

Accordingly, three contingency plans of 'Operation Crossbow'[5] were prepared by me in consultation with our officers and the same were subjected to detailed discussion and scrutiny by all the members of the Committee on 16th and 17th June, 1967 and finally approved by them after going through almost every word and line, making any alterations which they considered appropriate. At my insistence, the Committee members had to put their signatures on the plans in token of their approval so as to avoid any future misunderstanding. And my hunch proved correct sooner than I had expected! Incidentally, all these meetings and discussions were attended by the DIG, Jalpaiguri Range (SC De Chowdhury), the Deputy Commissioner of Darjeeling district (Manamoy Bhattacharya) and myself, besides the Addl SP, the ADM and the local SDO and SDPO.

The last paragraph of the Plans of 'Operation Crossbow' was titled 'Appreciation' (of the overall situation), part of which read thus:

"(a) As regards the operation as in Part C of the Plan, the possibility of heavy casualties could not be ruled out in case of desperate and violent resistance by the offenders. (In such an eventuality), the casualty figures may run up to anything between 30 and 250, though every effort will be made to keep the casualty figures to the minimum".

On their return to Calcutta on the evening of 17th June, the Committee members submitted their report to the Cabinet, including a copy of the above Plan of Operation, bearing their signatures of approval thereon! And quite a few cabinet ministers exploded in amazement at their colleagues having signed the 'virtual death warrant' of 30 to 250 people!

So the SP was summoned to Calcutta and asked to be present in a meeting of the full Cabinet - obviously to be grilled by many of the cabinet ministers. Accordingly, I accompanied the Chief Secretary (MM Basu, ICS) and the IGP (U Mukherji, IP, JP) to the cabinet meeting room. As could be apprehended, I was being grilled in this cabinet meeting by some of the well-known stalwarts in the ministry (notably by Somnath Lahiri, the veteran and respected leader of the CPI and Subodh Banerjee of the SUCI) to the effect that most of them had faced during their struggle of the past decades the ferocity, brutality and recklessness which marked large-scale police operations. In the light of their own past experience, how could I expect them to be a party to any such police operations which, inadvertently and unfortunately, some of their cabinet colleagues, i.e., the members of the Cabinet Committee which visited the district, had unwittingly approved.

Perhaps, much to the surprise and apparent embarrassment of the CS and the IGP, I stood up with an unexpectedly vocal riposte to the following effect: "Respected sirs, without in the least contradicting what all you have stated so far, based on your *past* experience, allow me to submit humbly that when you are talking about the *past*, I am talking about the *present and the future*. All your cabinet colleagues, the six honourable members of your Cabinet Committee, have not only seen for themselves but have painstakingly verified independently on the ground that not even one instance of the kind of brutality and reckless mayhem by police in the past referred to by some of you have so far taken place in the entire affected area of nearly 250 sq miles of Siliguri sub-division.

They have also satisfied themselves that we are genuinely unsparing and serious in our efforts to avoid any kind of bloodshed as may be humanly possible. And thirdly, sirs, your cabinet colleagues have also observed that a majority of the local villagers and other people of Siliguri sub-division in the vast area, irrespective of their political affiliations, are fully appreciative of the untiring efforts of the police and the local administration. Hence, I, as the person who prepared the basic draft plan of police operations for submission to the august body of six very eminent members of your cabinet, feel extremely distressed and anguished if our motives and the honesty of our purpose are called into question solely in the light of your experience of the past...".

The resulting tension in the cabinet room was all too apparent. At this stage it was Jyoti Basu (Dy CM) who intervened in his usual suave and balanced manner to defuse the tension by stating that the officers (meaning the Chief Secretary, the Inspector General of Police and myself) need not be present in the meeting any longer and that the final decision of the cabinet after further discussions would be communicated to all concerned within the next 2-3 days. This was my first exposure to Jyoti Basu's uncanny skill at crisis management and conflict resolution. Subsequent narration will show that even when Jyoti Basu was at the height of his power and glory during 1977-2002 as the Chief Minister of West Bengal, with his widely acknowledged all-India stature, part of which I had the opportunity of observing from fairly close quarters, both in Calcutta and in Delhi, he maintained this equanimity and characteristic poise and dignity.

There was only one casualty during the two major police operations, known as "Operation Hatighisa" of 12th July, 1967 and "Operation Buraganj"[6] of 13th July, 1967, which were personally supervised by me as the SP assisted by a number of other senior police officers; furthermore, nearly 95 per cent of the large body of extremists arrested during these two operations were released *on the spot* after some preliminary questioning and none, including those finally arrested and taken into custody was ill-treated, not to speak of any kind of brutality and use of third degree. Much later though, most UF leaders including Jyoti Basu generously acknowledged that the painstaking efforts of all ranks of the police during those and subsequent police operations vindicated the SP's assertions in the cabinet meeting of July, 1967.

In view of the heavy strain on me as the SP of Darjeeling district (series of *bandhs* and tea garden strikes during 1965-66, the Naxalbari trouble of 1967-68 and handling of the devastating floods and landslides of

October 1968 and so on), the IGP was gracious enough to ask me where I would like to be posted next, quite an unexpected gesture. I simply thanked him and stated that I would be happy to be placed in any capacity that he and the government wished. Eventually, I was posted as the Deputy Commissioner of Calcutta Police in-charge of its Security Control Division dealing with all categories of foreigners in West Bengal. It was a relatively light charge but with the highest special pay then and a good bungalow as official residence at Pretoria Street. So I joined as the Deputy Commissioner of Security Control (DC, SC) on 23rd January, 1969.

Dilemma over collecting Intelligence about Ruling UF Parties

It was too good to last long and soon thereafter, I was again in the thick of an emerging critical situation. After a spell of President's Rule, mid-term elections for the WB Assembly took place in February 1969 when the UF came back to power with an overwhelming majority. The CPM having won the largest number of seats, Jyoti Basu as the leader of its legislature party could easily stake his claim to be the Chief Minister. But, quite wisely, he allowed Ajoy Mukherjee, the veteran Gandhiite leader of the Bangla Congress, to be the Chief Minister. Jyoti Basu became the Deputy Chief Minister in-charge of the Police and the Home Department. The United Front obviously did so as a matter of political sagacity and compulsion of the new experimentation of 'United Front' government.

A month or two after joining as the DC, Security Control, I received a telephone call from the Commissioner of Police, Calcutta (PK Sen, IP, JP) who verbally communicated the government's order asking me to immediately take over charge as the Deputy Commissioner of Police, Special Branch (DC-I, SB) of Calcutta from its present incumbent 'because of some allegations of serious irregularity on the part of the latter'. I was also asked to report compliance within the next day or two. For the next 5-6 months, however, I had to hold dual charge as the DC, Security Control and the DC-I, SB till my formal release order was issued by the Government of India, the post of DC, SC being on the roll of the Central Government.

It was widely known that the Special Branch of Calcutta and its counterpart, namely, the Intelligence Branch (IB) for the rest of West Bengal, had been collecting intelligence on behalf of the government through their known mechanisms of human intelligence – through their long-term agents and short-term informers/contacts etc. and also through surveillance and interceptions, besides information available from published materials.

Interestingly enough, the Special Branch inherited till then as a legacy of the British colonial rule, a 'Kabuli Inspector', a Pushtu-speaking officer (Inspector Peshwara Singh, a Sikh gentleman) whose task was to collect information about the large body of Pathan and Afghan people inhabiting Calcutta, who were mostly engaged in the money-lending business besides a few traders in dry fruits and *hing* (asafoetida) originating from those areas from where the Pathans/Kabulis had come to Calcutta. Fortunately for us, importation of and peddling in narcotic drugs had not yet emerged as a profitable proposition for such people.

Intelligence collection in the above manner since Independence covered both open and secret activities of all political parties (including the ruling party, namely, the Congress) and their front organisations. Now that virtually all the political parties, barring the Congress, were part of the new government, the Intelligence Branch and the SB were in an obvious dilemma: should they continue with their past practice of 'covering' all political parties or adopt some fresh guidelines in the light of the changed situation.

At my request, rather insistence, a meeting was held between the Commissioner of Calcutta Police, the Deputy Inspector General of Police incharge of the West Bengal Intelligence Branch and myself as the DC-I, SB. One view was that the old practice should be followed 'quietly'. But I felt that howsoever 'quietly' it was proposed to be done, the continued wide coverage of all such parties and their front organisations, now forming part of the new government, cannot remain a secret for long, more so when many of our reports have to be sent to the State government (Chief Secretary/Home Secretary/Inspector General of Police and in some matters even to the Chief Minister and the Home Minister) and in some cases to the Government of India (through the Subsidiary Intelligence Bureau/SIB or directly to the Intelligence Bureau of the Ministry of Home Affairs in New Delhi). Then, in the not too distant a future the government and the ruling parties would accuse the IB and the SB of 'acting behind their back to subvert the new government', more so in view of their known 'sensitivity' about the IB and the SB!

Hence, I requested the Commissioner of Police and also the DIG, Intelligence Branch (WB) for a meeting to chalk out the line of our action as also its mechanism in the matter of intelligence collection and its dissemination to the appropriate authorities in the state and Central Governments. During discussions on 19th June, 1969 onwards, with the DIG, IB (WB) and the Commissioner of Police, Calcutta about the above dilemma of Special Branch and correspondingly of the WB Intelligence Branch as well, it was clear to me that none of my superior official was prepared to bell the cat – none of them was willing to even broach the subject either before the Chief Minister Ajoy Mukherjee or the Deputy Chief Minister and Home Minister Jyoti Basu. Noticing their reluctance to take the initiative in this sensitive matter, I proposed that, if they had no serious objection, I would like to place the cards squarely before the government and seek a clear mandate about the role and functions of the Special Branch. I also submitted that the West Bengal Intelligence Branch may like to do so in conformity with our basic functions, namely, intelligence/information collection and their dissemination to appropriate quarters on matters pertaining to –

(a) prevention of communal or sectarian strife,

(b) maintenance of public order,

(c) prevention of sabotage or damage to vital installations,

(d) keep watch over suspected subversive elements working at the behest of foreign governments and/or their agencies and, finally,

(e) forewarn the government in the state and/or at the Centre about elements which may be considered to be acting in a manner which may pose a threat to internal security, territorial integrity and sovereignty of India.

The West Bengal IB decided to play safe and cautioned me about such a 'risky venture' of formally writing to the government. Nevertheless, I decided to go ahead and seek a clear-cut mandate from the government about the role and functions of the Special Branch so that we did not have to act or do anything, even seemingly behind the back of a lawfully established government. Hence, I carefully prepared a Top Secret Note on the subject which was sent by me to the Chief Secretary and the Home Secretary, endorsing copies to the Commissioner of Police and the DIG, IB (West Bengal).

As could be expected, this created a flutter and within a couple of days, I was summoned by Chief Minister Ajoy Mukherjee and Deputy Chief Minister Jyoti Basu. The latter was particularly outraged at my 'unusual' request 'to cover the activities of even the ruling parties including their front organisations' and demanded to know why was it at all necessary ?

The three basic points made out by me in my Note and again verbally elaborated to them were to the following effect:

(1) The IB and the SB made no distinction in the past between ruling and opposition parties in regard to intelligence collection covering their five basic functions (as outlined in (a) to (e) above) and it would be in the interest of any government to allow such tasks to be performed by us.

(2) Furthermore, most of the enumerated tasks are obligated to be discharged by any lawfully established government and all its agencies, including the intelligence agencies, either under the common laws or under the Constitution and as such cannot be avoided.

(3) Moreover, would the newly formed government not be interested in knowing if any person or

persons or organisation, irrespective of their political affiliation, indulged in activities which could be reasonably considered to be aimed at subverting the lawfully established government of West Bengal or the Government of India? If the answer was in the affirmative, it should be one of the tasks of its intelligence agencies to collect the requisite information/intelligence and pass on the same to the government in an appropriate manner and in due time.

I concluded my submission by stating that if at any stage the government had reason to believe that the SB was not discharging its functions objectively and impartially, and in a professional manner, the government would always have the option of replacing me as the Deputy Commissioner incharge of the SB.

After my submission as above, it was Jyoti Basu who spoke to the following effect in his usual precise manner: "Even presuming that the CM and I may largely agree with your proposition, ours is a coalition government of so many parties and we have to function on the basis of consensus on important matters. So we have to place your Note before our cabinet and we can expect very strong views on such a sensitive issue. Though the CM and I would do all that we can, I am afraid that you may have to appear before the cabinet to defend your viewpoint and also assure them as to how you propose to prevent misuse of such wide powers".

Facing the Cabinet Again

As was expected, I was summoned, a couple of days later, to be present at the full cabinet meeting, along with the Chief Secretary and the IGP, to face the inescapable barrage of questions from quite a few of the cabinet ministers representing various political parties of the United Front. While confronted by some of the important cabinet ministers, I largely confined my basic submissions to the three points mentioned above and also elaborated on how we proposed to prevent any misuse or abuse of the charter of functions enumerated in my Note to the government. At this stage and to diffuse the mounting tension among his cabinet colleagues, the Dy CM Jyoti Basu intervened to make a statement somewhat on these lines: 'The CM and I have questioned the DC, SB at great length on this subject because I too had reservations about approving such a charter for the SB which would also be applicable to IB, West Bengal. But after discussions with the DC, SB, we felt that it would be in the interest of our government and the country to approve the proposal, with such safeguards against misuse as we may consider appropriate'.

Perhaps Jyoti Basu clinched the issue by further stating that most of the cabinet ministers of this second UF government were also in the cabinet of the first UF government who had "observed that the current DC, SB, who was the SP of Darjeeling District during the critical Naxalbari days of 1967-68, had performed his difficult duties with due restraint and responsibility. Any hasty, precipitative action on his part then could have led to the premature disintegration of the first United Front government. Hence, there was no reason why we should not trust his judgment as DC, SB now".

This intervention of Jyoti Basu quickly brought to an end the otherwise stormy cabinet meeting. Perhaps for the first time in the history of the Special Branch, Calcutta (and the Intelligence Branch, West Bengal), a clear-cut and written charter of functions for the Calcutta Special Branch and correspondingly for the West Bengal Intelligence Branch was formally approved by the government at the highest level. This also showed that Jyoti Basu was not merely a politician of long standing but was also emerging as a truly good administrator capable of taking fairly quick decisions and that too without beating about the bush.

Jyoti Basu aghast at his erstwhile comrade Ananta Singh's criminal deeds

There was a series of daring bank dacoities and time bomb explosions in Calcutta during 1968-69. It transpired later that all these dacoities used to be meticulously planned by the old revolutionary Ananta Singh of the well-known Chittagong Armoury Raid Case (April 18, 1930), then in his eighties! And the time bomb explosions were caused by a young couple who happened to be close allies of Ananta Singh before they dissociated themselves from Ananta Singh. It started with the Park Street Post Office dacoity case, followed by the Grindlay's Bank dacoity (twice in two different branches), Park Street Branch dacoity of the State Bank of India and so on.

There was no breakthrough in any of the bank dacoity cases and the Commissioner of Police was under considerable pressure from the Governor, Dharma Vira, during President's Rule. To make matters worse for the Calcutta Police, a series of time bomb explosions also took place during the period at the US Consulate, the American Centre, the General (Head) Post Office and in a number of posh cinema halls of Calcutta (Metro, Lighthouse, Elite, Globe, etc.) which used to screen English mostly Hollywood movies. As was the practice in Calcutta Police, all these cases were being investigated by teams of experienced investigators of the Detective Department (DD) of Calcutta Police under the direct supervision of the Deputy Commissioner of Police-I, DD, Debi Roy.

Since there was no breakthrough in the investigation of any of those sensational cases of daring dacoities and time bomb explosions during the past one year or so, there was considerable public criticism, resulting in further pressure from the government on the Commissioner of Police and the Detective Department of Calcutta Police. Perhaps to deflect the growing public criticism against the persistent failure of the famed Detective Department of Calcutta Police, in addition to the continuing pressure from the Governor, the Commissioner of Police, PK Sen, IP called me to his office and desired that some of those cases should be investigated by the Special Branch under my supervision.

I told him fairly clearly that the Special Branch of Calcutta Police had never dabbled in or investigated criminal cases since Independence in 1947, its ambit being collection, collation and dissemination of intelligence on matters related to aspects of public order, VIP and internal security. As such, the SB officers had no expertise in criminal investigation. The CP agreed with my contention but nevertheless insisted that I should be incharge of the supervision of all these cases and I could draft any of the SB officers whom I wanted to be associated with these investigations and that the services of the officers of Calcutta's Detective Department along with its Deputy Commissioner (being junior to me) will be placed at my disposal. I felt this proposition of the CP, though generous enough, would not be a workable solution for various reasons. Finally, I submitted to him that it would be in the fitness of things to have a composite team of DD and SB officers under a joint team with the Joint Commissioner of Police (KB Chakraborty, a former DC, DD), myself (DC-I, SB) and the DC-I, DD, Debi Roy. My suggestion was readily accepted by the CP and the Joint Task Force as above was formed the same day. And this new venture in due course proved to be a great success, thanks to the self-effacing manner in which the Joint Commissioner of Police, a highly competent and truly professional police officer, helped in building up a good team spirit with specially selected investigators from the DD and the SB. Debi Roy and I too struck up an excellent rapport which lasted against all odds.

How and who to bell the cat?

Our joint efforts could eventually lead to Ananta Singh as the mastermind ('High Command') but there was till then no hard proof or evidence to pin him down. He also happened to be an important leader of the CPM at one time and known to be an old colleague of Jyoti Basu. A series of our raids led to recovery of an unexpectedly valuable document, containing the detailed plan of the Park Street State Bank dacoity and that too in the handwriting of Ananta Singh. To further strengthen our hands, our joint team considered it necessary to 'monitor' Ananta Singh's telephone calls.

However, by then the second UF government had come to power and the new government had put an embargo on any phone tapping without the specific order of the government, which meant clearance from the Chief Minister or the Dy CM as the Home Minister. But who will dare to bell the cat, asking Jyoti Basu to allow us to mount an electronic surveillance on his erstwhile comrade's telephone. The CP and the Joint CP desired that this unpleasant task was to be performed by me.

Hence, I obtained an appointment with the Dy CM without fully disclosing the purpose of my meeting with him but only stating that there were some important developments in the bank dacoity and time-bomb explosion cases which needed to be brought to his notice. By then, our Special Branch officers had succeeded in picking up the young couple who perpetrated the time bomb explosions. Painstaking interrogation revealed that the duo had initially been a part of the Ananta Singh gang but later got disillusioned with the 'high command', left the group but decided to organise 'actions against the US imperialists'. Their targets included the US Consulate, American Center as well as some wellknown cinema houses in Calcutta which used to screen Hollywood films.

I met the Dy CM equipped with the statements of the couple and the very vital Park Street State Bank dacoity plan in the handwriting of Ananta Singh. After briefing him about the developments in the investigation of all these sensational dacoity and time bomb explosion cases, it was mentioned that many of the suspects in those cases had been arrested by then but the 'real culprit and the mastermind' had not yet been touched. The Dy CM enquired why this person could not be arrested if our investigation pointed to his involvement. I mentioned at this stage that this person was somewhat of a VIP in the political spectrum of the CPM and that he had been in the habit of flaunting his proximity to Mr Basu. "Who is this great fraud who had been, as you say, exploiting my name and our party's name?" Then I mentioned that this person was the legendary Ananta Singh whom, as children, we adored as one of the heroes of the famous Chittagong Armoury Raid of 1930s!

Mr Basu was aghast at this revelation and wanted to know if we had any clinching evidence against this person. I was literally waiting for this opening, and enquired if he was acquainted with Ananta Singh's handwriting. His reply was that even though he had not seen his handwriting during the past few years, it should be possible for him to recognise the same. When the Park Street State Bank dacoity plan, with minutest details for the operation, all in the handwriting of Ananta Singh, was shown to him, he was shocked but immediately recognised the handwriting as that of Ananta Singh, and reacted strongly by saying that he could never imagine that this person with such glorious past had turned into such a criminal. He also readily admitted on his own that he and a few others in the CPM were growing increasingly suspicious about some of the strange behaviour patterns of Ananta Singh, some of which he narrated to me to bring home his point.

The Dy CM then enquired as to what we proposed to do to this person in this regard. I stated that we would have to arrest him but only after collecting some more circumstantial and corroborative evidence and for this we had to start monitoring his telephone calls. His unambiguous response was for us to go ahead. But I reminded him that in view of the new government's existing embargo on telephone tapping, in spite of a provision in favour of it in the Indian Telegraph Act, we could take up the tapping operation only after obtaining the Government's clearance to that effect in writing and that too solely for the purpose of investigation of a series of serious criminal cases i.e., bank dacoity and time bomb explosion cases, etc. which we had already registered. It did not take Jyoti Basu long to decide in favour of the above course of action. In fact, he asked me to prepare a self-contained note on the matter and bring the file to him personally with the CP's recommendation thereon. This was done within the next couple of days and the Dy CM did not prevaricate and gave his approval thereon 'as an exceptional measure and in the interest of investigation of some serious criminal cases'.

As mentioned earlier, the CP, the Joint CP as well as the DC-I, DD, Debi Roy, had understandable reservation about Dy CM's reaction to our request for such a drastic departure from the new government's ban on telephone tapping and that too in respect of a 'legendary' person like Ananta Singh. My gut feeling, however, was that if the facts were put across to Jyoti Basu in a straightforward manner and without any hidden agenda or motive, he too will react in a straightforward and decisive manner. And I was proved right, much to the surprise and relief of the Commissioner of Police, PK Sen and Joint Commissioner of Police KB Chakraborty who was the leader of our joint investigation team.

It goes without saying that tapping of the telephone of Ananta Singh produced some startling disclosures pointing to his further plan to sell his fortress-like house in Garia area, a suburb of Calcutta, for shifting to a 'safe haven' in Mumbai very early as he had correctly suspected that his role in the series of dacoities had been exposed and that he was apprehensive of his arrest. In due course, and not too long thereafter, Ananta Singh's house was raided by our team including the Joint CP, myself and DC-I, DD along with our key investigators, which made headlines in the newspapers for quite some time thereafter. Ananta Singh was duly put under arrest, produced before the magistrate who remanded him to our custody for a certain number of days. Under government order, Ananta Singh was detained under the Defence of India Rules (DIR).

The WB Assembly elections were held on 9th February, 1969 and formation of the second UF government took place soon thereafter with almost the same political parties as in the case of the earlier UF government of 1967. As an aftermath of the victorious euphoria, the militant cadres of some of these parties, notably of CPM and SUCI, were physically assaulting unarmed policemen of the subordinate ranks in particular, apart from humiliating them in public in various manners. Such episodes obviously led to considerable resentment and tension among policemen. These incidents were taking place mostly in the districts of 24 Parganas, Howrah and Nadia, the traditionally violence-prone districts. Unfortunately, the police in these areas did not take effective steps either to prevent the recurrence of such incidents nor did they take steps to assuage the understandably hurt feelings of the policemen under their charge.

In one such incident of unprovoked violence against policemen, a constable of the 24 Parganas District Police was severely assaulted and virtually lynched by such party cadres. This happened in an area now under the district of South 24 Parganas. The highly agitated policemen of the area brought the body of the slain policeman to the Police Lines of the District HQ at Alipore where the office of the SP and most other senior police officers of the district were located. Within a short while, several hundred agitated policemen congregated there and started shouting slogans, demanding urgent steps to stop such atrocities against the police. There was a virtual police rebellion, which was further aggravated by the SP of the district who, instead of facing them or trying to assure them of suitable action against the culprits, escaped from his office by the backdoor. This obviously added fuel to the fire and the rebellious mood got aggravated.

Though the 24 Parganas District Police was a part of the West Bengal Police and not of the Calcutta Metropolitan Police, Alipore Police HQ of the district was located within the Alipore police station area under the Calcutta Police jurisdiction. Hence, the above information reached me at around 1 pm and I immediately went over to the next building, 13 Lord Sinha Road, HQ of the West Bengal Intelligence Branch, since the 24 Parganas District Police was part of West Bengal Police but the above agitation was taking place within the Calcutta Police jurisdiction, met the DIG IB Ranjit Gupta and informed him about the seriousness of the Alipore developments. He immediately called for the senior most Special Superintendent of IB, WB, SK Sinha who was told by his DIG that no information had reached him till the DC SB informed him about the situation.

Therefore, two IB officers were forthwith sent to the spot to ascertain the facts and to report the developments. Meanwhile, when all three of us – DIG, IB, SS-I, IB and myself – were trying to ascertain more details and possible consequences, SB's Divisional Intelligence Officer (DIO) incharge of Alipore PS area SI Prabhabesh Chatterjee continued to keep me informed over phone all developments and was also keeping the Calcutta Police HQ Control Room at Lalbazar informed of all the above developments in accordance with the standing instructions and practice of the SB in situations of threat to public order and peace. Besides, I was also invariably ringing up the Commissioner of Police and the senior officers at the Lalbazar Control Room (three Deputy Commissioners of Police on special duty), informing them about the rapidly developing situation.

Rebellious Policemen invade the Assembly House

Eventually, the angry and rebellious policemen (approximately 200, some carrying their rifles) decided to march to the Writers' Building, the seat of state government, to seek redressal from the highest quarters of the government. On the way, they realised that the Assembly was in session where the Chief Minister, the Deputy Chief Minister and others would be present. Hence, instead of proceeding to the Writers' Buildings, they barged into the Assembly House compound, shouting slogans against Jyoti Basu and Hare Krishna Konar, another important CPM leader. I was with the DIG, IB and his SS-I when the information reached me from the same officer of SB. After informing the CP and the senior officer in the Control Room about the 'invasion' of the Assembly House by a group of angry policemen, many of whom were armed, I decided to proceed straight away to the Assembly House.

It took me hardly twenty minutes to reach the Assembly House, where I found groups of highly agitated policemen, some with rifles. In order to find out what exactly had happened inside the Assembly Hall, I rushed in there, to be greeted with an eerie silence, with only 3 or 4 MLAs in the hall, the rest having 'escaped' at the earliest possible opportunity. I still recall the presence of the three

Jyoti Basu, Deputy Chief Minister, Nalinaksha Sanyal, an elderly and respected Congressman of long standing and Pannalal Dasgupta, an erstwhile revolutionary of the RCPI. I requested all three of them to accompany me to the Deputy Chief Minister's chamber within the Assembly building. I could get hold of one sergeant and two constables of Calcutta Police on duty near the Assembly Building gate and put them in front of Deputy Chief Minister's chamber, with strict instruction not to allow anybody to enter this room till I return. Then I informed Jyoti Basu that I would try to meet the agitating policemen within the Assembly compound, talk to them so that the tension among them could be reduced to the extent possible and bring some of them to Dy CM so that he too can assuage their hurt feelings.

Meanwhile, the Commissioner of Police, PK Sen, 2-3 Dy Commissioners of Police as also the DIG, IB/WB RK Gupta along with some other senior police officers of WB Police had arrived in the Assembly complex and all of us were doing our best to bring down the tension. Till then, I had no occasion to inform them that the Dy CM had been safely lodged in his Assembly chamber and kept under guard to prevent any harm to him.

By then the agitating policemen must have started realising that in their anger and frustration they had done something which would disgrace the entire police force. I could get hold of some such policemen within the Assembly compound and started talking to them in the following vein, after disclosing my identity as DC, Special Branch: "One can understand the totally unjust and unmerited attack and humiliation of policemen by some anti-social elements within the ranks of one or two of the ruling parties; senior police officers of your district should have taken all possible steps to ensure that policemen were not victimised; at the same time, whatever has happened on this day including your 'invasion' of the Assembly house was bound to divert public and official sympathy into strong public disapproval".

While I was talking to the initial group on the above lines, many more of the rebellious policemen gathered around us and I could make out that the rebellious mood was changing for the better. Luckily for me, some of them could also recognise me as the previous SP of Darjeeling district whose handling of the Naxalbari movement had brought a fair degree of public and official approbation for policemen of all ranks. Two of them, in particular, who appeared to be among the leaders of this outburst in the 24 Parganas district Police Lines, ultimately leading to their hasty 'invasion' of the Assembly House, came out by asking for my advice as to what can be done to prevent their 'victimisation'.

I was perhaps hoping against hope just for a breakthrough. I said that some of us would plead with the government and senior police officers to ensure that there was no attitude of vindictiveness among the senior officers and the government. But as a first step and to strengthen our hands, I was prepared to take 3 or 4 of them to the Chief Minister or the Dy. CM so that they may briefly narrate the type of attacks and humiliations they had been suffering at the hands of the criminal and anti-social elements of various ruling parties, and putting forward simultaneously their requests that (a) the government should do all that was necessary to prevent their humiliations and attacks against them in future, and that (b) they regret whatever had happened at the Assembly complex. In addition, I also volunteered to request the government to see that there was no victimisation. These policemen appeared to be in agreement with my suggestions. Thereafter, I took these 4-5 policemen to Jyoti Basu's chamber and requested him to allow these policemen to express their grievances and viewpoints as also their suggestions and requests to him.

When I lodged him in his chamber, after rescuing him from the Assembly Hall, Jyoti Basu was a totally shaken person, obviously realising that such a large body of rebellious policemen, many of whom were carrying rifles, could be up to any kind of mischief. But when I returned with a small body of policemen after about 15-20 minutes, he had regained his self-confidence and his skill in management of a crisis situation. He stood up from his chair and started speaking in a fairly firm and confident manner, somewhat on the following lines: "Whatever you people have done today, especially within the sacred precincts of our Assembly building, has disgraced the entire police force and the government. We will have to deal with this very firmly because that is what all the MLAs are bound to demand. If you had legitimate grievances, could you not convey these through your official channels and in a disciplined and civilised manner"?

Presuming that such utterances of the Dy CM may further aggravate the already surcharged mood of the rebellious policemen, I intervened at this stage to say that most of the rebellious policemen, as I could gather during my interaction with them a short while ago, regretted at whatever had happened. But for the time being, the Dy CM may kindly allow the representatives of these aggrieved policemen to express their grievances. Jyoti Basu, being a sharp judge of men and situations, must have realised that some opportunity needed to be given to them now itself to let out some steam, so to say. And before the Dy CM could respond to my suggestion, I asked the police leaders that one of them may briefly speak about their grievances and that later they can give in writing to the IGP their grievances and suggestions. Having gone through this exercise by two of the representatives of the angry policemen for about 10 minutes or so, I thanked the Dy CM for his patient hearing, informed him that he may kindly stay back in his chamber till I returned to him, and promptly took the policemen out of the Dy CM's chamber but telling them that it would be their moral duty now to ensure that all their associates vacate the Assembly compound as quickly as possible and return to their respective units and places of work, informing them that their views and grievances have been conveyed to the highest level of the government and that all concerned will try to ensure that their legitimate grievances were duly redressed early and that too without any victimisation.

Shortly thereafter, the Commissioner of Police, DIG (IB, WB), some officers of Calcutta Police along with me escorted Dy CM Jyoti Basu to his chamber at the Writers' Buildings. Besides us, the Chief Secretary, the IGP, the Home Secretary and SM Murshed, Joint Secretary, Home, joined soon for an emergency meeting. The Commissioner of Police reiterated his apologies and regrets for their failure to prevent the forcible entry of the rebellious policemen inside the Assembly precincts and their subsequent misconduct 'for lack of any prior information'. I had no option but to refute the CP's statement and briefly stated my conversations with the senior officers incharge of the Control Room that day (DC,

HQ / DC, SC and DC, AP) as also with the CP himself twice, all of which took place in the presence of the DIG, IB and the SS-I, IB while I was in DIG, IB's room but CP repeated that they had no information. I only stated that it would be possible for me to adduce proof of 'whatever' I had said. The Dy CM then wanted to know whatever the IGP and the DIG, IB had to say.

I knew the CP, PK Sen, to be a straightforward gentleman, not given to pettiness or guile. Hence, I felt that there must have been a lapse of memory on his part, for whatever reason, and that the three senior IPS officers at Lalbazar Control Room on that day must have misled the CP to cover up their own serious lapses. I also had an uncanny feeling that some gross mismanagement on the part of the three senior IPS officers on special duty that day must have taken place at Lalbazar Control Room and that I must find out at the earliest opportunity what exactly had gone wrong there.

Three DCs at Lalbazar Police Control Room caught in flagrante

The meeting at the Writers' Buildings was still on though it had shifted to the room of the Chief Secretary. I excused myself for a short while and asked my friend Murshed to accompany me urgently on a fact-finding purpose at Lalbazar Control Room. It took us hardly ten minutes by car to reach there. We went straight inside the Control Room. The scene which greeted us was really bizarre–the three senior officers (DCs HQ/Security Control/Armed Police), who were jointly holding charge of the Control Room (C/R) on the fateful day, were busy altering two vital records of the C/R–the Telephone Log Book and the General Diary which recorded all incoming and outgoing calls and their corresponding entries in the General Diary! They were literally caught in flagrante.

At my instance, Murshed in his usual blunt manner and after uttering a few expletives 'seized' all those documents the originals as well as the partially tampered ones ! These reflected all the calls made by me and my SB officer, with their timings and gists thereof. By the time Murshed and I returned to the Writers' Buildings, the meeting in the room of the Chief Secretary was over and I requested Murshed to keep the 'seized' records in his personal custody as these would be very vital for any inquiry into the incidents of that day which the government would surely order.[7]

CP's urgent meeting early next morning

On reaching home that day around 10 pm, I was informed by the Control Room Duty Officer that the CP had convened an urgent meeting in his room early next morning, which was to be attended by me, the Joint CP, DC, HQ and the two other DCs who were on duty in the Control Room. In this morning meeting, the CP asked all the three DCs who were in the C/R on the previous day, to try and recapitulate whatever they were in the know of, all the three DCs routinely denied having received any message or information from the DC, SB or his officer or from any other quarters. All three of them were seated in front of the CP whereas the Joint CP was on his right and I was on the left. CP's telephones, 5 or 6 in two rows and his scribbling note-pad too were on CP's left, almost in front of me!

While the three DCs were making their submissions one by one, my eyes chanced upon two or three scribblings in CP's note-pad and in his handwriting (in Bengali): "*Jyoti Basur mundu chai / Harekrishner mundu chai*" (We demand the heads of Jyoti Basu and Harekrishna Konar). The CP again mentioned his ignorance about any alert message either from the C/R officers or from any other quarters. At this stage, I came out with my submission, based on the following two points: firstly, if the three DCs in the C/R had not received any calls either from my officer, Prabhabesh Chatterjee, or from me during the entire duration of the turmoil, what prompted them to start altering the Control Room's Telephone Log Book and General Diary entries of the day? Then I mentioned, for CP's information, the surprise visit to the C/R last evening by Murshed and me and 'seizure' of the original as well as the fabricated records and their contents as well. The CP was truly aghast and shouted at the three DCs who were on special duty in the Control Room on the previous day for having kept him totally in the dark about this important development.

The second point of my submission was based on the two entries in CP's note pad and in his handwriting, which were lying in front of me, regarding Jyoti Basu and Harekrishna Konar and I put my finger on these slogans being repeated by the rebellious policemen, which were mentioned, among other developments, both by my officer and me to the C/R DCs and also to the CP by me at least twice around lunch time while I was still in the room of the DIG, IB. For some moments, the CP closed his eyes and then burst out, shouting against the DC (HQ) and the two other Control Room DCs for totally misleading him and feeding him falsehood: "This is for the first time that my memory played tricks with me and I thank Arun for helping me in recapitulating the course of events, including the exact words spoken to me by him over telephone..." This was the straightforward PK Sen that I had known!

Later in the evening Murshed mentioned to me over phone that he had already narrated to the Dy CM about the previous evening's visit to Lalbazar C/R by the two of us and also showed him the 'seized' documents and their contents. The Dy CM's response to this, as mentioned to me by Murshed, was characteristically brief and succinct: His gut feeling was that the DC, SB would not have misled them and that he must have narrated the true picture.

Transfers and postings of police officers

One hears a lot about 'political pressure' in the matter of transfers and postings of officers, including in the police. This is especially so in respect of police officers of various ranks, more so regarding the crucial and cutting edge levels of OCs of Police Stations (Sub-Inspector or Inspector), SPs of districts and also in respect of some other higher level posts.

Let there be no mistaken notion that such things happen only in the police department. Such a 'disease', as I call it, covers virtually all levels and all segments of administration. Even the Education departments, primary, secondary, higher secondary, colleges and universities, with a few individual and honourable exceptions, suffer from such a pernicious disease–something which was unthinkable and unheard of, at least in West Bengal even in the fifties and sixties of the last century. There is no point in blaming the ministers and other political leaders for such a state of affairs–a section of officers is equally, if not more, to be blamed for this malady. On completion of my deputation to the

Government of India–first as a senior faculty member (1972-74) of the National Police Academy, then in Mount Abu, and later as the DIG of CBI's largest branch, Delhi Metropolitan Branch, from July 1974 to early 1980, I was posted as the Resident Representative of the West Bengal Industrial Development Corporation and concurrently Joint Resident Commissioner of West Bengal. The then Chief Secretary, AK Sen, was gracious enough to offer these posts so that we could stay in Delhi to allow our two sons to complete their college and school education respectively and also for my wife to continue with her teaching assignment with a college of Delhi University.[8]

In early 1983, I was promoted and posted as the Special Inspector General of Police (HQ). In that capacity, I had to oversee and assist the State's police chief, DGP, on law and order matters but was also tasked with the responsibility of ordering transfers and postings of police officers of and below the rank of Inspectors, who were Gazetted Class-II officers in West Bengal.

A few days after I had assumed the above charge, I received a telephone call from a heavy-weight West Bengal cabinet minister not to transfer a certain Inspector of Police from a North Bengal district. That Inspector had a known bad reputation about his integrity. Hence, my response to the minister was quite sharp: "Sir, I am not aware of any government order which authorizes you to order/suggest where our officers are to be transferred or posted, especially when the officer concerned has a bad reputation about his integrity". "On top of that", I further stated, "that the officer has been holding on to a 'lucrative' post far beyond the stipulated period. Hence, I regret that I cannot entertain your request'! Saying this, I put down my telephone receiver, walked into the DGP's room next door and narrated to him what had transpired between me and the minister.

The DGP was aghast at my strong riposte to the minister and said something to the following effect: "Arun, this would lead to avoidable confrontation with the minister who, apart from his official portfolio, was incharge of the North Bengal districts; moreover, you have been somewhat out of touch with the affairs of the state for nearly eleven years, being on deputation with the Government of India". And my response to him was somewhat on the following lines: "It would be OK with me if you ask the government to shift me to some other post but I would not be party to a situation wherein senior officers are required to abdicate their lawfully enjoined duty and responsibility and be dictated to by political leaders, 'ministers or otherwise..."

As I returned to my room, I received yet another telephone call from the same minister, whose commanding tone had changed by then and he asked me if I could come over to his room for a cup of tea or coffee, I responded by saying that I was attending to some urgent matters and would be able to drop in after about fifteen minutes or so. Eventually as I entered the minister's room, I found the Secretary of his department, RN De, a senior IAS officer of good repute, present there. Surprisingly, the minister got up from his chair, shook hands with me and enquired if I would like to have tea or coffee! When I opted for coffee, he ordered coffee for the two of us, the minister and me, and informed his secretary that he would resume further discussion of the departmental subject in the afternoon.

As we were sipping coffee, the minister started by saying that he had just learnt from his secretary that I was the same officer who had been a very successful SP of Darjeeling district who not only dealt with the onset of the Naxalite movement and many other difficult situations during 1965-68 and had earned the respect of the people. When I enquired as to how he knew all this, he mentioned that during those years he was himself a middle-level party and trade union leader in the adjacent Jalpaiguri district.[9]

After such 'preliminaries', he reverted to the case of the Inspector of Police against whose transfer order he had spoken to me. The minister said that the concerned officer was honest and hard-working which prompted him to take up the cause of the officer. My response was on the following lines: "Sir, as a veteran politician and an important minister, you would know that the Enforcement Branch (EB) of police unfortunately has a very bad reputation, even amongst policemen! There are undoubtedly many good and honest persons in EB but the officer mentioned by you is not only known to be a dishonest one but, secondly, he had managed to stay put as an Inspector of the same District Enforcement Branch much beyond the stipulated 2-3 years and had developed vested interests there. As such I had no option but to transfer him from his present post but also to a non-DEB assignment".

I must say to the credit of the minister that he did not try to make an issue out of it. In due course, I kept the DGP and the Chief Minister informed of the above development. Though my DGP was somewhat crestfallen, the CM's response was that I had acted correctly. He further stated that on an appropriate occasion, he would again tell his ministers and party leaders not to interfere in routine transfers and postings, though they can bring to the notice of the senior officers concerned any case of alleged grave injustice but leave the final say to the judgement of the senior officers. I wonder if the CMs of any other states would have reacted in a similar manner!

Sometime after I took over charge as the Special IGP (HQ), I received a typed but unsigned sheet of paper from the CM's office, containing names of about 10-15 police officers of various ranks, Sub-Inspectors, Inspectors, Dy SPs, SPs and even DIGs. It showed their places of postings and also their proposed postings. I enquired from the officer of CM's personal section who brought the list to me as to whether the list was seen by the CM before being delivered to me and his answer was in the affirmative. One look by me at the list made me feel that it might have been shown to the CM but he had obviously not applied his mind or did not know much about the professional and general reputation of the listed officers.

Hence, I just put the date on which the list was given to me, went over to the DGP's room, showed it to him, mentioning about its origin and enquired as to what I was supposed to do since I had genuine misgivings about most of the names of the officers in the list. The DGP reiterated his earlier homily that 'I was out of touch with reality, having been away from the state for nearly eleven years' and that I was expected to issue suitable orders in respect of the officers of and below the rank of Inspector and then pass on the list to the DGP for necessary follow-up actions, through the Home Department.

I realised that the DGP was not prepared to bell the cat and wanted an easy way out. Hence, I did not pass any orders nor did I pass on the list to the DGP. Nearly two months had elapsed thereafter and I could sense the restiveness of many of the tainted officers, who had obviously worked through various political and other channels for the expected 'lucrative' postings which were nowhere in sight. So they reactivated their known channels for early issue of orders and consequently the pressure on the CM was obviously increasing. Inevitably, one day I received a call from the CM's office, wanting me to meet the CM. When I did so the same day, after making sure that none else was in his room, the conversation was somewhat on the following lines:

CM: "Did you receive any paper from my office regarding transfers and postings of police officers and what was the position?"

Spl. IGP(HQ)/APM: "Yes sir, I did receive a typed list but I could not pass any order thereon because most of the recommendations were in respect of known dishonest or utterly incompetent officers and that too for being placed in known 'lucrative' posts. This fact deserved to be brought to your notice before I acted on the basis of the recommendations. However, I have already started the process of collecting and collating all available information about these officers, based on their service records, annual confidential rolls and otherwise too from various credible sources. If you kindly give me two days' time, I would be able to put across to you all the relevant facts in writing".

The CM said that I could meet him with relevant papers at 9 am in his official residence at the Raj Bhavan Annexe building on the third day. I went there on the appointed date and time and handed over to him a 10-12 page note, containing the names of the officers, their places of existing and recommended postings as also details about their service records including their reputation regarding honesty and integrity. After carefully going through each page of my note, the CM finally came out with an anguished expression: As you are already aware, I do not know any of these officers. The list was compiled in my office on the basis of recommendations received from many of the Left Front ministers and some from important LF party leaders. The compiled list was shown to me before being sent to you or your DGP for orders and other necessary follow-up actions, as was the earlier practice.

I am glad that you have not issued any orders in view of the hard facts mentioned in your tabulated statement. It is for the first time that the real facts are being brought to my notice. Can you give me a copy of your statement so that I may bring such distressing facts to the notice of our ministers and party leaders, asking them to carefully scrutinise and cross-check facts about the credentials of officers before making any such recommendations in future?

I had gone to meet the CM with four copies of my scrutiny report, two of which were handed over to the CM for such action as he deemed proper. The same day I handed over one copy to my DGP, with a supplementary note indicating the details of my meetings with the CM as well as his responses thereon. I could discern in the DGP a mixed feeling of surprise, at my audacity and relief at the CM's response.

Let me add as a footnote to this episode that it did not take long for words to get round that such practices would not go unchallenged in future – not by the then Special IGP (HQ) at least. I wondered then, and I do so even now, as to what would have been my fate if I had dared to ignore the CM's recommendations in some other states?

Handling of complaints from CM's influential CPM party leaders against the young Sub-divisional Police Officer by Jyoti Basu

The young and newly inducted IPS officer, Sanjoy Mukherjee, IPS/1989, was holding charge of a fairly turbulent and violence-prone Barrackpore sub-division in the district of 24-Parganas. After studying the situation on the ground closely, he observed that most of the cases of violence and criminal activities were being perpetrated by the anti-social elements, mostly under the umbrella of the ruling parties. This prompted him to organise Operation Sashtra, i.e., recovery of illegal arms, ammunitions and explosives, followed by arrest of those elements responsible for acts of violence and anti-social activities.

Hence, the young SDPO's Operation Sashtra started having the desired impact on the ground, prompting many such elements to flee from Barrackpore sub-division to escape arrest by the police. Inevitably such elements approached their mentors, dadas, in the ruling parties, who went on a delegation to meet the CM with a written memorandum of complaints and also demanding immediate removal of the SDPO.

All these and much more I learnt from the CM himself! Let me go back a little in time. About two years after my retirement from the IPS on January 1, 1992, I was somewhat taken by surprise when the CM conveyed his desire that, because of my CBI background, he would like me to take charge of the somewhat non-functional Vigilance Commission of West Bengal very early. Till then this post was generally filled up by a retired Chief Justice or a Judge of Calcutta High Court or by a retired Chief Secretary of the state. Obviously a certain section of the bureaucracy felt either apprehensive or unhappy, or both, at such a move by the CM and, therefore, no formal order was being issued.

After about a month, the CM wanted to know whether I had assumed charge as the Vigilance Commissioner. I responded by stating that no such order had been received by me and, therefore there was no question of my assuming charge. Jyoti Basu smelt a rat and could see through the delaying tactics of the higher echelon of the bureaucracy. Late that evening the CM's Personal Secretary rang me up to say that the CM had ordered the Chief Secretary to issue the appropriate order and also to ensure personally that the order was delivered at my Salt Lake residence the very next forenoon. And that had to be complied with. The Chief Secretary also contacted me over phone to convey the above instruction of the CM and requested me to take charge as the state's Vigilance Commissioner the very next day 'as desired by the CM'!

Within a few days after assuming charge, it was clear to me that hardly any department bothered to give effect to the VC's recommendations. In most cases even the elementary courtesy of sending a suitable reply to the Commission was lacking. All important vigilance cases and recommendations thereon were supposed to be monitored by the Chief Secretary but in reality nothing of the sort was in evidence in real terms.

When I brought to the notice of the CM such a sorry state of affairs, he wanted to know what could be done to improve things. I suggested that every three months, the VC should meet him along with the Chief Secretary to bring to his notice the progress, or the lack of it, on the part of any department and seek his orders thereon. The

CM readily accepted my suggestion and desired that the Chief Secretary may also be informed of this arrangement as approved by him.

As the Chief Secretary and I went to CM's room for one such review meeting, sometime in mid-September, 1993, I was taken by surprise at what the CM narrated then: "You never told me that your younger son Sanjoy Mukherjee was an IPS officer of our state, who was then the SDPO, Barrackpore?.".. I stated that "Sanjoy literally joined West Bengal on the day I retired as DGP. Even otherwise, sir, it would not have been proper on my part or even fair to the young officer to mention to you that the new IPS entrant in WB was my son. But, sir, I am somewhat curious to know why, in the first place, you asked me this question?"

The gist of what the CM stated then was somewhat like this: "It is common knowledge that Barrackpore sub-division is a troublesome and turbulent area. About 5-6 weeks back some of the important CPM and other Left Front leaders of the area, including two MPs and 3-4 MLAs came to me in a delegation with a long memorandum containing their allegations against the SDPO.

The allegations pertained to the new SDPO's actions, mainly directed against their party (CPM) cadres whose houses were raided, many of them arrested and the rest had to flee from the subdivision for fear of being arrested. Hence, the delegation members demanded that this officer deserved to be not only transferred immediately but also suspended for such 'selective' and 'harsh' actions against CPM Party cadres".

How did the CM react to such a fairly high-powered delegation of his own party? I can almost quote his words:

"I took the memorandum and asked the leaders to contact me after about 7-10 days as their allegations, including their demands for the SDPO's removal and suspension were serious matters of administration and I would have an early inquiry made before initiating further actions... Thereafter I sent one copy each of the memorandum to the Chief Secretary and the DGP, asking them to report the result of the inquiry within a week.

I also gave one copy of the memorandum to our Alimuddin Street party office, asking for an inquiry by a responsible party leader not belonging to Barrackpore sub-division and to send me a report within a week.... When all the three inquiry reports as above came to me, I was rather surprised to note that there were many common points–that the SDPO's reputation about his integrity was unquestioned, that he was personally leading most of the raids, that these raids unearthed very substantial quantities of illegal arms and explosives, that a very large number of criminal and anti-social persons were arrested and that many of those arrested were known to be our party's 'supporters' and so on...As you know, such bad elements generally flock under the ruling party's umbrella for their protection.

But equally, if not more significantly, all the three reports mentioned that (a) the reputation of the officer about his personal integrity was unquestioned, (b) that such efforts of the young IPS officer led to unearthing of considerable quantities of illegal arms and explosives, (c) these actions had already produced substantial improvement in the law and order situation in the entire subdivision. On top of all these, the reports also mentioned that (d) the long-standing grievance of the local people about eve-teasing and harassment of innocent persons had been completely stopped due to the untiring and sustained efforts of the SDPO, much to the relief of a very large number of families of the entire subdivision..."

The CM continued thus: "...At this stage I came to know that this IPS officer was your younger son. After going through all the three reports, I did two things: Firstly, I told the Chief Secretary, who was in CM's room along with me that day, that this officer should not be transferred as asked for by some of our party MPs and MLAs and that this officer can be transferred only when the officer was due for promotion and that too after consulting him (i.e., the CM). Secondly, I told our party leaders that the delegation leaders/members who gave me the memorandum with incorrect and distorted facts about a young, honest and hard-working officer deserved to be cautioned..."

I still wonder how many Chief Ministers in our country, not to speak of one of Jyoti Basu's stature, would have shown such magnanimity and maturity of judgement to protect the reputation and honour of a young officer, even against the demands of a vocal and powerful section of his own party leaders.

References

1 In those years, Inspector General of Police and the Commissioner of Police (Calcutta) were vested with some magisterial powers and as such were known as Justices of the Peace (JP) and since they belonged to the British era of Imperial (later Indian) Police, hence they used the appendage IP in place of the later day Indian Police Service (IPS).

2 This book was written by me during the Naxalbari days (1967-68) but published in 2007 by M/s KP Bagchi & Co., Kolkata-700 012 and was formally released in June, 2007 at the Conference Hall of the Vigyan Bhavan Annexe, New Delhi.

3 Refer to pp. 131-32 of *Maoist Spring Thunder*, op. cit. The IGP's observations were prophetic as was seen in hindsight and in later decades - from Lalgarh (Paschim Midnapur) and the rest of Jangalmahal in West Bengal and elsewhere in Srikakulam, Karimnagar of Andhra Pradesh, Dantewada of Chhattisgarh and its adjoining Gadchhiroli of Maharashtra as well. Likewise, parts of Bihar, Jharkhand and Odisha are also experiencing the Naxalite upsurge even now, perhaps in a more virulent form than in West Bengal. It merits mention here that in recent times, some idealistic and well-meaning District Collectors like Alex Paul Menon of Sukma district of Chhattisgarh, besides many other devoted police officers of various ranks like in Odisha, West Bengal and in other states continue to be mercilessly butchered and blown off by the Naxalites/ Maoists on the utterly misplaces pretext of ushering in peoples' revolution!

4 This 6 member Committee consisted of some of the important leaders of the coalition partners, namely, Harekrishna Konar of CPI(M), Biswanath Mukherjee of CPI, Sushil Dhara of Bangla Congress and a close confidante of Chief Minister Ajoy Mukherjee, Nani Bhattacharya of Revolutionary Socialist Party (RSP), Amar Prasad Chakraborty of Forward Block (FB) and Deo Prakash Rai of All India Gorkha League (AIGL).

5 Details of the plan called "Operation Crossbow," may be seen in the author's book titled *Maoist Spring Thunder*, op. cit., pp. 104-15.

6 Details of the large-scale police operations, especially of 12th and 13th July, 1967, known as the "Operation Hatighisa" and "Operation Buraganj" respectively may

be seen in the author's book titled *Maoist Spring Thunder*, op.cit., pp. 112–16.

7 The government set up within a few days a one-man Inquiry Commission with R Gupta, ICS (retd), former Chief Secretary ...and a person of unblemished reputation for integrity and professionalism. Mr Gupta carefully recorded the statements of virtually all the persons connected with that day's incidents, starting with the SP of 24 Parganas district, DIG, IB (WB), the SS-I, IB (WB), DC-I, SB, Sub-Inspector Prabhabesh Chatterjee of SB, all the three DCs on special duty in the Lalbazar (Calcutta Police) Control Room along with some other officers on duty at the C/R, Commissioner of Police, a DC and some other officers of Calcutta Police who were on duty at the Assembly (outside/inside) and SM Murshed. The Inquiry Commission's report strongly indicted the SP of 24 Parganas district; the DIG, IB, CP, Calcutta and the three DCs of C/R also came in for severe critical observations. The role played by the DC, SB and his Officer SI Prabhabesh Chatterjee was highly praised 'for their performance of professional tasks with commendable care and promptness, even in the midst of chaos all around'.

8 I could thus continue in Delhi till early 1983, by which time our elder son Amitabha had joined St Stephen's College of Delhi for his graduation with Economics Honours and our younger son Sanjoy completed his schooling in St. Columba's and later joined the Presidency College in Calcutta as a student of Economics (Hons); later he did his MBA from IIM-Calcutta. In due course, Amitabha joined the IAS in 1983 and Sanjoy joined the IPS in 1989.

9 I learnt subsequently that he was a bachelor and an honest person even after remaining as an important minister of the West Bengal cabinet till his death a few years later.

Chapter 2

Rajiv Gandhi

The 'Black Wednesday': 31st October, 1984

It was indeed a 'black day' in the history of post-independence India just as the day on which Mahatma Gandhi, the apostle of peace and non-violence was fatally shot by a fanatical Hindu. The 'Black Wednesday' on 31st October, 1984 saw the assassination of the then Prime Minister Indira Gandhi by two fanatical men who, ironically, were her security guards.

During the forenoon of the 'Black Wednesday', I as the Special Inspector General of Police (HQ) was busy holding an important meeting with my officers. In the midst of the meeting, I received a call from the DGP in the next room, asking me to come over immediately. From his tone over phone, I could make out that something was amiss, but I was totally unprepared for what I gathered from him; the DGP had just received a call from the Ministry of Home Affairs in New Delhi that Prime

Minister Indira Gandhi was shot at in the compound of her official residence at Safdarjung Road in New Delhi and that she had been rushed to the All India Institute of Medical Sciences (AIIMS) with serious gun-shot injuries. The officer from MHA asked the DGP to immediately inform her son Rajiv Gandhi, who was on a political tour of West Bengal, to return to New Delhi urgently and that a special aircraft was being sent to the Dum Dum Airport in Calcutta to bring him back to Delhi.

We knew that Rajiv Gandhi was then holding public meetings in far away Contai subdivision of Midnapore district, a few hundred kms away from Calcutta. The information from Delhi was immediately brought to the notice of the West Bengal Chief Minister Jyoti Basu, the Chief Secretary and the Home Secretary and the other follow-up steps which we proposed to take, requesting the Chief Secretary to tie up with the Kalaikunda Air Force Station in Midnapore District for urgent despatch of two helicopters to Digha or Contai where landing facility would be available. We also spoke to the District Magistrate and the SP of the district, requesting them to ensure that the above information was urgently conveyed to the persons concerned, also stating that the state government was arranging despatch of two helicopters from the nearby IAF base at Kalaikunda to ferry Rajiv Gandhi and his companions from Digha/Contai to Dum Dum Airport.

After making these arrangements, I accompanied the WB DGP, RK Bhattacharjee, to Dum Dum Airport to ensure that all arrangements at that end were in order. The special plane from Delhi, we were informed, would arrive at Dum Dum Airport within two hours. We checked with the Control Tower of Dum Dum Airport but they had no information till then about the exact time of arrival of the aircraft. With the help of the chief of the Dum Dum Airport Authority, we got an Indian Airlines plane off-loaded, cleaned up, refuelled, provisioned, security-checked and kept as a stand-by near the VIP bay. The Airport Authority was also requested by us to make alternative arrangements for the scheduled passengers so that they are not stranded indefinitely. Just around that time, two helicopters with Rajiv Gandhi and his entourage, Pranab Mukherjee, Arjun Singh, Priya Ranjan Dasmunshi, Mani Shankar Aiyar and some others, touched down at the Dum Dum Airport.

I still vividly recall the scene: Rajiv Gandhi in his usual white *kurta-pajama* and a tricolour *khadi* scarf wrapped round his neck, unusually red in the face, obviously due to inner tension and emotion on hearing about the news of his mother having been shot, and a small transistor radio held in one hand close to his ear, desperately trying to get the latest news about his mother's condition. We briskly walked towards him, and he too was coming hurriedly towards us, to further convey the Delhi message, stating that till that moment the Dum Dum Air Traffic Control Tower had not been able to establish contact with the special plane from Delhi supposed to be here during the next hour or so.

Rajiv Gandhi kept asking if we had any further information about his mother's condition and we could only say that the PM had been rushed to AIIMS and was being attended to there. We also informed him that we have commandeered an Indian Airlines plane which had been refuelled, security checked and kept nearby. He did not want to wait for the Delhi special plane and decided to leave immediately by this stand-by plane arranged by us locally with the help of the Airport Authority. He and his entourage were promptly ushered into the plane in which the right-hand front row was kept reserved for Rajiv Gandhi, who beckoned Pranab Mukherjee (presently President of India) to sit by his side. As far as I recall, the others in the entourage included Arjun Singh, Priya Ranjan Dasmunshi, Mani Sankar Aiyar and a few others. Within about ten minutes the plane took off on its way to Delhi; and the special plane from Delhi touched down about an hour later thereafter.

The DGP and I witnessed some disturbing signs while we were returning from the Dum Dum Airport to our Police HQ in Writers' Building. There were attempts at road blocks by Congress workers and others to protest against the dastardly attack on PM Indira Gandhi. We got down from our car at several such places along the road, asking the people to refrain from any such activities. On reaching the Police Headquarters, both of us spoke to a number of Congress leaders of West Bengal, requesting them to restrain their workers from any rash actions.

We felt that some more concrete steps were needed to be taken from our side to prevent any communal, anti-Sikh outbursts in any part of West Bengal:

(a) We alerted the Calcutta Police on this matter for introducing suitable preventive measures throughout the city, including continuous road patrolling by police wireless vans and special watch over areas having substantial Sikh population.

(b) Then we spoke to all our SPs of the districts for immediate actions on the following lines, among others:

- To introduce mobile two-way road patrols along all national and state highways to ensure that there could be no attacks against Sikhs driving trucks or any other vehicle.
- Trucks being driven along the highways and other roads were to be marshalled in bunches and to be kept by the side of the highway under armed guards to prevent any attacks against them.
- The dhabas run or frequented by Sikh drivers and others also to be kept under guard or frequently patrolled by armed mobile vans.
- Gurdwaras and Sikh residential areas to be equally subjected to frequent watch and patrolling by armed policemen.
- District and subdivisional Police Control Rooms to be asked to monitor the above measures frequently and keep the Control Room at State Police HQ informed of all developments.

My later diary entry for this tragic day read as follows:

"Assassination of PM Indira Gandhi at 1, Safdarjung Road residence, New Delhi (shots fired at 09.20 hours by two of her security guards (Sikhs)....16 gunshots... Though believed to have died on her way to AIIMS, official announcement made later... She would have been 67 years in November this year...A most dastardly act and a blot on us as a nation – the Sikhs would take long to live down this shame and the fanaticism displayed in this sordid episode... Rajiv Gandhi sworn in (in the evening) as Prime Minister: a perfect gentleman – should make his mark as an outstanding PM. May he live long!"

Did I have any premonition on that fateful day which prompted such a spontaneous prayer on my part for Rajivji's long life? I do not think I had any such dark thought even in the remotest corner of my mind, but I did know that when fanaticism of this sort grips the mind of any individual, group or class of people, rationality and sanity become the instant casualty.

There was another diary entry on the night of 3rd November (1984): "Funeral ceremony of Indira Gandhi: Truly a day of national mourning. She had achieved many things as PM. Let us hope and pray that her untimely death will not be in vain, and will strengthen the forces of unity, secularism, democracy and socialism. A remarkably composed and dignified bearing of Rajiv Gandhi as could be observed on the TV during his mother's funeral and thereafter. May he live long and bring greater glory to India!"

However, as a former Deputy Commissioner of Police of Special Branch (Calcutta) and thus responsible for VIP security including the PM's security on her visits to Calcutta, especially during the Bangladesh liberation struggle of 1969-72, the thought did cross my mind that those charged with the onerous responsibility of VIP security, especially of the new Prime Minister Rajiv Gandhi, will have an extremely difficult and critical task and that the slightest lapse in this regard may be disastrous for our country. Jyoti Basu, as the Chief Minister of West Bengal, fully shared my views and anxieties. Perhaps this prompted him to ask me to supervise the security arrangements in Darjeeling for our new Prime Minister Rajiv Gandhi during the latter's first visit there on 6th December, 1984.

What Jyoti Basu stated thereafter was quite unexpected: "I am told that Subash Ghising[1] still remembers you as the old *SP-sahab* of Darjeeling and that people there also have considerable respect for you. As such, your presence there may be helpful in ensuring that the militant elements among the GNLF and others do not pose any threat to the security of our young Prime Minister..."

Gorkhaland Agitation in Darjeeling Hills

The Hill people of Darjeeling district, popularly known as the Nepalis or the Gorkhas, have been traditionally appreciated all over our country as disciplined, law-abiding, fun-loving people and fiercely loyal to India, with a strong martial tradition–somewhat like the Sikhs of Punjab. As the SP of Darjeeling district for over three years (1965-68), I developed a special love, affection and admiration for the people of all the three Hill sub-divisions, Darjeeling Sadar, Kurseong and Kalimpong. My wife and I developed a special bond with many of these Hill people, common men and women as well as the eminent ones like Tenzing Norgay, of Mount Everest fame, his nephew Nawang Gombu, another Everester and a host of other residents of this district.

An unknown youth leader known as Subash Ghising emerged, as if from nowhere, as a firebrand youth activist in 1966 and I had occasion that year to protect him once from being physically assaulted by an angry mob of the Hill people for some 'indiscretion' on his part. After being in virtual hibernation for over a decade and a half, he re-emerged as the chief of a newly formed separatist organisation known as the Gorkha National Liberation Front (GNLF). In December 1983, he was reported to have addressed a letter to the King of Nepal seeking support for a separate and independent state of Gorkhaland. He thereafter wrote in a similar vein to the United Nations, the President of the USA and to several other heads of States. Obviously, there was no response from any of those quarters.

Gradually, Ghising succeeded in mobilising a sizeable section of the youths in the Hill areas on the emotive issue of a separate state and embarked on the path of armed confrontation with the state administration. This prompted the West Bengal Chief Minister Jyoti Basu to deprecate Ghising and the GNLF as 'anti-people, anti-national and secessionist', whereas some in the Government of India misled Rajiv Gandhi into believing Ghising as a 'patriot and a nationalist'. The Central Intelligence agencies could not have been unaware of the patronage, financial and otherwise, extended to the GNLF by a powerful person in the royal palace in Nepal and also about similar encouragement from another foreign government.

The central agencies utterly miscalculated the entire situation, presuming that the GNLF could be bolstered as a counterpoint to the Left Front Government of West Bengal in general and the CPM in particular. There could not have been a worse miscalculation and a dangerous one at that from the national security point of view. The WB Intelligence Branch and its very dedicated Darjeeling District Intelligence Branch (DIB) had excellent sources of Intelligence not only in the Hill areas but also in the adjacent areas of Nepal from which we knew about (a) GNLF's extra-territorial connections and patronage, (b) its bank accounts in Nepal, and (c) the name and other details of Home Ministry's link with Subash Ghising, obviously operated through one of the Central

Intelligence agencies, many of whose top-level leaders as also quite a few of their operatives in West Bengal were known to me.

I had reason to suspect that some of the top officers in the Central Intelligence agencies had been trying to ingratiate themselves with the PM by giving him a distorted picture of the movement – that the GNLF agitation would seriously erode CPM's support base among the Hills people and also cause considerable loss of its credibility in the plains of West Bengal districts. With my background knowledge of West Bengal, the strengths and weaknesses of the CPM and its Left Front and the psyche of the Bengalis, I knew for certain that the Left Front and the CPM may lose one parliamentary seat and at most three assembly seats in any election in the near future.

But they will more than make up for such loss in the rest of West Bengal and that the net loser will be the Congress. And this is precisely what happened later - the Darjeeling Lok Sabha seat was won by the GNLF candidate Inderjit Khullar, Home Minister Buta Singh's emissary, foisted by one of the Central Intelligence agencies, and the three assembly seats of Darjeeling Sadar, Kurseong and Kalimpong. But in the Plains districts, the CPM and the Left Front could more than make up for this loss and eventually weaken the Congress even in some of their traditional bases.

I was not concerned with the political fall-out of New Delhi's manipulative moves but felt that they were playing with fire, trying to foment alienation where it did not exist and in the process were also likely to cause severe strain on our national security aspect. As a professional policeman, I felt outraged at this kind of manipulative and ill-conceived moves by the Home

Ministry, duly aided and abetted by some people in the Central Intelligence agencies. I was quite confident that if an unbiased and objective picture could be brought to the notice of the young Prime Minister, who was neither a petty nor a 'veteran' politician, he would take suitable corrective steps.

Accordingly, I decided to pay a 'special' visit to Delhi to convey the appropriate 'message' to the PM and contacted over phone from Calcutta the Director, Intelligence Bureau, HA Barari, known to me at least since 1969-70, for an early meeting with him to discuss some 'sensitive and disturbing aspects' of the ongoing GNLF agitation. He could sense the urgency and perhaps guessed what I was up to, knowing me as he did. The suggested meeting took place a few days later, on September 4, 1986 in the DIB's chamber in North Block, with a sumptuous lunch thrown in! The only other person present during this meeting was the then Additional Director of the Bureau MK Narayanan[2], an old friend of mine also since 1969-70; his sharpness of intellect, the ability to comprehend and his power of articulation were simply unparalleled. I was obviously very happy when later he became the National Security Advisor (NSA) in the Government of India (2008).

I spoke to them rather bluntly about the ill-conceived moves being made from New Delhi, as observed by us, after briefly mentioning Ghising's Nepal and later his New Delhi connections and his sources of finance including some bank accounts known to us. Considering the strategic importance of Darjeeling district and the loyalty, honesty and simplicity of the Hills people of Darjeeling, all of which I had known intimately from my days as the SP of Darjeeling district and thereafter.

I strongly felt that no one, either at the Central or state level should even attempt to 'play politics' with these people, which they genuinely detested. All that these people expected was that they should be treated fairly and justly, which they really deserved. As such I had been feeling rather disturbed, I mentioned, when it came to our notice that some people in Delhi including perhaps some in the Central Intelligence agencies were indulging in petty, partisan political manoeuvres which would not only be politically counter-productive but may as well imperil the national security in the long run.

My final observation was somewhat on the following lines: "I do not really know for certain whether some RAW operatives or Intelligence Bureau operatives, or both had been involved in this situation but my earnest request through the two of you i.e., DIB and Addl DIB, is to ensure that such operatives must de-escalate and that the Prime Minister be adequately advised to enable him to play a constructive role in defusing the tension in the Hills region".

Within a month or so, we were observing signs that my meeting in North Block had not gone in vain even as the Prime Minister was periodically showing signs of personal interest in defusing the tension. For some months during 1984-86, Jyoti Basu as the West Bengal Chief Minister and Prime Minister Rajiv Gandhi were making public statements contradicting each other's stand over the GNLF issue. But soon a de-escalation process coupled with a search for arriving at some common ground became discernible. Its reflection was also there on the GNLF leadership's utterances which were no more strident nor were their cadres indulging in overt violent actions.

Jyoti Basu and Rajiv Gandhi

The final healing touch took place at Darjeeling Raj Bhavan on February 9, 1987. A few days prior to that, we received the Prime Minister's schedule of visit to Darjeeling and Jyoti Basu was especially invited by the Prime Minister for GNLF related discussion with him at Darjeeling Raj Bhavan. I could gather from the Chief Minister as well as other sources that this meeting of 9th February was going to be a crucial one. Surprisingly, the Chief Minister desired that I should be available at the Raj Bhavan while he would be meeting the Prime Minister on one-to-one basis – just in case he needed clarification or further information on any point since I was closely monitoring the GNLF agitation on behalf of the state government almost since its inception in 1984.

However, I had a hunch that some breakthrough in the continuing stalemate could be expected, though its full picture appeared somewhat murky till then. The picture became clearer and the jigsaw puzzle in my mind was resolved when I saw Inderjit Khullar as an 'unobtrusive' person, trying hard to be a part of the VIP entourage and being literally sneaked into the Raj Bhavan along with an 'operative' of a Central Intelligence agency(!) and a few GNLF leaders including Subash Ghising!

At the Raj Bhavan, Rajiv Gandhi and Jyoti Basu were closeted for about an hour of one-to-one discussion. When the two of them came out in the adjacent hall of the Raj Bhavan, Subash Ghising came there accompanied by two or three of his lieutenants, virtually ushered in by Inderjit Khullar. Ghising came forward to greet the Prime Minister in their traditional manner by handing over to him a *khada*, a kind of raw silk scarf, and the PM shook hands with him. Jyoti Basu was standing on the

PM's left and I was standing one step behind the PM and Jyoti Basu. Rajiv Gandhi's reaction thereafter was typical of him – spontaneous, generous and gentlemanly: "Mr. Ghising, you now greet your Chief Minister in the same manner as you have done to me" and it looked like catching Ghising on the wrong foot and making him do just as the Prime Minister had wished. Ghising placed a similar *khada* in the hands of Jyoti Basu and mumbled a few words of greetings to him, who too reciprocated in his usual suave manner. Till then the two of them, Chief Minister Jyoti Basu and GNLF supremo Subash Ghising, were not on talking terms. At last the ice was broken to the relief of everybody, thanks to Prime Minister Rajiv Gandhi's thoughtful gesture!

Then started the process of dialogue, firstly, between the Chief Minister of West Bengal and the Union Home Minister Buta Singh, finally culminating in 1987, with the full backing of Prime Minister Rajiv Gandhi, in the Darjeeling Gorkha Hills Council (DGHC) Accord. Ghising was made its Chairman and substantial functional autonomy was given to the DGHC in respect of a number of items till then within the exclusive domain of the state's administrative jurisdiction. The Council was also granted liberal financial assistance both by the Union and the state Governments. This was made possible by the statesmanship of both Rajiv Gandhi and Jyoti Basu but for which the GNLF episode would have caused considerably lasting alienation among the Hills people of Darjeeling district[3].

As desired by the Chief Minister, I was in Darjeeling on December 4, 1984 itself renewed all my earlier contacts that could be of considerable help in diffusing the tension in the area, at least during Rajiv Gandhi's first visit to Darjeeling as a Prime Minister. A rehearsal of the police, including security, arrangements was held on 5th December at Lebong helipad area, along the line of route up to the North Point School ground and its vicinity–along the route of the Prime Minister's visit. The PM's visit on 6th December, 1984 was a great success, with thousands of men, women and children in colourful attire and in a festive mood, who thronged around the Lebong helipad area and all along the road from there to the PM's public meeting venue at the North Point School ground. To everyone's surprise, we could mobilise even a good number of trustworthy volunteers from amongst the GNLF who were also very useful in maintaining peace along the line of PM's route and also at the public meeting venue of the PM which was marked by an unprecedented turnout of women, children including school students attired in their respective school uniforms.

My diary entry for December 6, 1984 reads as follows:

"After having met Rajiv Gandhi on the fateful October 31, 1984 when we ushered him and his entourage into the IAC plane at Dum Dum Airport for being taken to Delhi, 6th December, 1984, this was the first occasion when I had the opportunity of meeting him as our new PM–perhaps the most handsome, vibrant, forward-looking and young PM that India could boast of as we all had occasion to observe in the following years. It was an immensely satisfying moment for all of us, especially for me".

Rajiv Gandhi's visit to West Bengal

The continuing perception of threat to his security was uppermost in my mind when the VIP security role had to be assumed by me as the Special Inspector-General of Police, Intelligence Branch (West Bengal) during 1986-87 for all the hectic tours of West Bengal by our new Prime

Minister - either to visit some remote rural areas of West Bengal, perhaps as part of his planned 'familiarisation' with the remote rural areas or of the flood-affected areas of West Bengal or on the eve of the 1984 Lok Sabha elections or the 1987 Assembly elections in West Bengal.

As was expected, the Lok Sabha was dissolved and the Election Commission declared 24 and 27 December 1984, as the dates for the Lok Sabha polls and the counting of votes was to start on 28th December. This meant a period of hectic election campaign by all concerned including Prime Minister Rajiv Gandhi who had to do it all over the country. So far as West Bengal was concerned, his election meetings were scheduled for 17 and 18 December. As the IGP [HQ] then i.e. 2-I/C to the State Police Chief, it was my duty to remain in regular and daily contact with the districts to monitor the law and order situation including the security arrangements on the ground as also the electioneering by the various political parties, quite often leading to needless frictions.

The election meetings of the young Prime Minister were drawing unprecedented crowds. On December 17, 1984 he held public meetings at Budge Budge [crowd strength approximately 70,000], Canning [25,000], Haroa [60,000]. No one could imagine that the last two, in the fringe areas of the Sunderbans, could attract such huge crowds. In the midst of his hectic campaigning, Rajiv Gandhi visited Belur Math, headquarters of the Ramakrishna Mission. His public meetings in Calcutta proper, which were slated for the afternoon and the evening, were equally spectacular: Deshpriya Park [18,000], Park Circus Maidan [20,000] and Deshabandhu Park [65,000]. His itinerary for poll campaign for December 18 included Howrah [30,000], Burdwan

[18,000] and Asansol [65,000] in West Bengal and then he moved to Bihar.

It is, of course, a matter of history that the December 1984 Lok Sabha elections resulted in the highest-ever number of seats obtained by the Congress Party, or for that matter any party or combination of parties since 1984. "Out of the 542 Lok Sabha seats, the Congress got 415 seats, with 48.1 per cent of the votes. Since then, and even during the Nehru-Indira periods, the Congress never could obtain so many seats and this was largely due to the strong 'sympathy wave' in favour of the Congress[4].

The sympathy wave in the wake of the brutal assassination of Indira Gandhi did make a considerable impact but that by itself could not account for such a phenomenal success unless one also takes into account the personal appeal of this new and young Prime Minister– his charisma, heightened by his smiling face, the personal warmth which he exuded all around him and, of course, a new kind of leadership which the people were wanting to discover.

If we fail to give due importance to the latter aspects as mentioned, we would not be able to explain the 1989 Lok Sabha elections result, the second half of which had to be concluded after the brutal assassination of Prime Minister Rajiv Gandhi on May 21, 1991 at Sriperumbudur near Chennai.

PV Narasimha Rao, a great scholar and one of the most astute politicians in India then, had to round up the second phase of the electioneering for the Congress Party to the best of his capability. But his party could just manage to scrape through with 218 seats despite the sympathy wave after Rajiv Gandhi's brutal assassination and the second half of the election taking place thereafter. After all, there could not be a second Rajiv Gandhi with all his unparalleled attributes as perceived by the mass of people!

Rajiv Gandhi's extensive tour of Bengal country side

On September 18, 1986 Prime Minister Rajiv Gandhi arrived at Calcutta and stayed at the Raj Bhavan after attending to his numerous engagements in Calcutta.

On September 19, 1986 the PM was scheduled to visit several places in the backward districts of Purulia and Bankura and thereafter visit Durgapur, Burdwan district, and Haldia, Midnapore district, where he was to address public meetings. It appeared that such unscheduled visits to interior villages and meeting people there, mostly the poorer sections, were perhaps a part of his mass-contact at grass-root level as well as familiarisation with rural India. Though this kind of schedule meant tremendous strain for the Prime Minister, besides over-stretching our security arrangements for the PM in view of known security threats, I kept wondering how many of our Prime Ministers would take such trouble and go through such a punishing schedule just to get to know the real face of rural India first hand!

Due to bad weather conditions, there was no possibility of helicopter flights either from the Royal Calcutta Turf Club (RCTC), popularly known as the Race Course, helipad at Calcutta or from Dum Dum Airport on the morning of 19th September. As such it was decided that the journey from Raj Bhavan to Dum Dum Airport would be by road, and from Dum Dum Airport to Jamshedpur (not on schedule) by an Avro plane, from Jamshedpur to Nimedih (also not on schedule!) in Bihar (now in Jharkhand and close to Purulia border of West Bengal) by helicopter. As the Special Inspector General of Police, Intelligence Branch (WB), I was tasked by the state and Central Governments to accompany the PM and party as the Chief Security Liaison Officer.

It was my first exposure to the young Prime Minister's penchant for ignoring quite a few of the Blue Book security protocol laid down by the Government of India. Firstly, the VIP i.e., the PM was not to be allowed to drive the car in which he was to travel.[5]

His favourite vehicle was a chocolate coloured Suzuki van (?), with a specially fitted ISUZU engine which made it an extremely powerful car capable of being driven at very high speed. This was air-lifted from Delhi along with an identical reserve vehicle. Much to my horror, the PM himself started driving this car from Nimedih and we entered into Purulia district of West Bengal. Ignoring the scheduled route of journey, which are invariably 'sanitised' from the security point of view, the PM started getting off the scheduled route and drove into interior village roads, driving up to the point to which the vehicle could be manoeuvred and then he walked up to the nearest village, unknown to even the district officers!

He used to talk to the villagers in Hindi to enquire about their problems relating to water supply, agriculture, sanitation, educational facilities for the children and so on. Quite often he entered some of the mud huts to have a look inside. After about 15-20 minutes in a village, he would move on to another village in a like manner, at times walking quite some distance to reach a village. I could see that, in spite of exerting himself to the utmost, this kind of a punishing schedule was a bit too much for the elderly Congress leader Arjun Singh accompanying him and he wisely sat down under a shady tree in the midst of a nowhere land; I requested him not to venture into what our young VIP was doing effortlessly, instructed one of our officers to look after him, saying that we will pick him up as part of the convoy when we return through this very stretch.

In other words, the whole security arrangement on the line of route went haywire, enough to give jitters to those incharge of PM's security. But I knew that *the element of surprise could be the greatest protection against security threats* and as such there was no point in unnecessarily making a fuzz about the line of route security.

After visiting quite a few of the unknown interior villages of Purulia district by road and on foot, we came to Purulia town with the PM's convoy for a brief lunch. He was again on the road and went through a similar series of unscheduled visits to unkown villages of Bankura district. Thereafter on the way to Durgapur in Burdwan district, his first public meeting as yet, his vehicle nearly overturned while crossing a small river, prompting some of his SPG officers and a few of us including the Director SPG, Devinder Singh rushing towards the vehicle, putting it on all four wheels and pushing it beyond the river bed–with the PM grinning all the way, as if to tell us that he was sorry to cause such 'unintended trouble' for us, whereas we were really concerned and anxious about his safety ! That was his way of disarming us with his impish but generous smile.

Finally around 5 pm, we made it to Durgapur, the steel town and a known bastion of the Leftist parties, especially the CPM. He addressed a huge crowd in his public meeting here. He was to finally retire quite late at night to the Tagore Guest House of Durgapur but only after the usual unending rounds of delegations not only from his party but also from other parties and their front organisations as well. It was well past midnight when we succeeded in persuading him to retire to his bedroom because we knew that tomorrow too would be a long day for him, more so when we had given up any hope of persuading him to be driven by the trained Police/SPG driver.

The next day, 20.09.1986, his convoy left Durgapur at about 6 am. That meant he could hardly sleep for 4-5 hours but in the morning he looked his usual self - fresh, radiant and smiling. The road journey from here to Panagarh airfield, Burdwan district, was not a long stretch and the journey from Panagarh to Indian Air Force base at Kalaikunda, Midnapore district, was by a Boeing aircraft. Then started the road journey to nearly seven interior rural areas of Midnapore district including Guptamani, Kashiapota, Keshiari, Egra and Mahisadal.

On the way to all these areas, he stopped at numerous unscheduled places, spoke to the villagers, enquiring about the problems faced by them in regard to their means of livelihood, family, state of health, sanitation, water supply and educational facilities for their children. We could see that he was not talking the usual jargon of politicians nor was he enquiring about the villagers in a cursory manner. The sincerity of his purpose was perhaps apparent to these ordinary and generally neglected villagers. It must have been so all over the country which he was trying to cover systematically during this 'familiarisation' phase of his tours.

The PM's convoy eventually reached the developing industrial and port town of Haldia, also in Midnapore district, around 3 pm. After hardly 10-15 minutes' break at the nearby guest house, he was ready to address a sizeable audience at Haldia. Thereafter another small stretch of road journey to Kukrahati for river crossing on to Diamond Harbour (6.30 pm) in the district of 24-Parganas, followed by nearly two hours of road journey up to Dum Dum Airport where from he took off for Delhi at about 20.30 hours of September 20, 1986.

The Prime Minister's next schedule of extensive visits to West Bengal was from December 18-20, 1986 arriving from Delhi at Dum Dum Airport at 9 am on 18th December. By 9.30 am his convoy was on the move, the first stop being at Barasat, 24 Parganas district, followed by Gaighata, Bongaon, Bagdah, Dutta Phulia, Bagula, Krishnanagar, Nadia district, Palashi and finally reaching Berhampore, Murshidabad district HQ, around 11 pm. Apart from the scheduled public meetings at most of the above places with unusually heavy turnouts of people, almost the entire stretch of the road of several hundred kms was thickly lined up by people from all walks of life and of all age-groups, male and female. Though it was a spectacular sight for all but for those of us - the SPG officers from Delhi and all of us from West Bengal Police charged with the extremely onerous security duty of the Prime Minister - could never lower our guard even for a moment.

Early next morning on December 19th, 1986, Rajiv Gandhi and those accompanying him including those charged with his security, left in two helicopters from a helipad at Berhampore and touched down at Malda. The road journey started after a public meeting in Malda town and then on to several other places in the districts of West Dinajpur and Darjeeling, where the Prime Minister also addressed several public meetings.

Prime Minister's *'vanishing act'*!

I am sorry to have caused you all such worry but the stretch of road was so nice that I could not resist the temptation of testing the capacity of my car's engine!

After a night halt at Darjeeling Raj Bhavan, the PM and party left around 7.30 am in two copters, touched down at Bagdogra[6] and again started a gruelling road journey, with public meetings at Siliguri and Jalpaiguri towns and several other places in the districts of Jalpaiguri and Cooch Bihar. The last public meeting was at Alipur Duars around 10 pm and from there, he was scheduled to travel by road to the Hashimara Airport (IAF).

Then followed *a thoroughly disturbing 'vanishing act'* indulged in by the PM! After the last public meeting at Alipur Duars in North Bengal, the PM's convoy was heading towards Hashimara around 10.30 pm. But after only a couple of minutes, the PM's car was nowhere in sight! Even the two SPG cars could not keep pace with the preceding car of the PM, driven by Rajiv Gandhi himself as was his habit despite our efforts to dissuade him. The SPG Director, Devinder Singh and I were travelling in the third escort car and both of us were equally worried because it was a dark night and most of the road was either a desolate stretch or having thick forest on both sides.

On my repeated contacts over the radio-telephone (R/T) with the officers in the Pilot Car and the Advance Pilot Car, all that we could gather was that the PM's car was not within their sight either, all that they could tell us was that one car in very high speed had overtaken both but due to the darkness and the high speed of the overtaking car, they could not enlighten us if it was the VIP car! All of us in the four protection/escort cars (2 of SPG and 2 of WB Police) had by then considerably increased our speed while moving towards Hashimara airfield. The gap between losing track of the PM's car and reaching Hashimara could have been about 10-15 minutes or so but it seemed like eternity, keeping all of us on tenterhooks and in deep anxiety.

I still recall vividly what was awaiting us in front of the airport's small lounge; Rajiv Gandhi was standing with a broad smile on his face, as if to 'receive' us near the entry gate! I could not restrain myself and immediately on getting out of our car I blurted out in genuine concern somewhat to the following effect: 'Sir, this is not to be done for reasons of your security and you do not perhaps know what anxious moments we had to spend on way to Hashimara...'. His response was an even broader smile, putting his hand on my shoulder, saying softly "I am sorry to have caused you all such worry but the stretch of road was so nice that I could not resist the temptation of testing the capacity of my car's engine! Now let's go inside the lounge where I have already ordered cups of coffee for us!" SPG Director Devinder Singh and I were obviously speechless after such a gesture of the PM and sheepishly followed him into the lounge. Within about half an hour of our arrival at Hashimara, the PM left for Chennai in a special aircraft which had arrived an hour earlier from Delhi with some persons who were to travel with the PM for some important discussion en route, which meant throughout the next two hours or so, after such a gruelling tour, the PM was not to have a wink of sleep well past midnight.

Despite the risks involved in doing so, I periodically reminded Rajiv Gandhi about our duty and obligation in respect of his security. I must admit that he never took exception to any of my candid views and suggestions but he had the most gracious way of disarming me with a benign smile or a kind word! At times, when Sarla Grewal, Principal Secretary to the PM, accompanied him, I could also request her to do all that was possible on her part to prevent any breaches of the mandatory security requirements by any person, including the Prime Minister, because his security risks, according to my perception, were bound to be of a very high order for all time and at all places. I will revert to this aspect later, but only as a sad postscript to the tragic Sriperumbudur episode.

On 23rd or 24th December, i.e. 4-5 days after the Prime Minister left the Hashimara airfield on way to Chennai around 10.30 pm, Grewal rang me up from Delhi to say that the Prime Minister had asked her to obtain from me a "Top Secret /for PM's eyes only" Note regarding various suggestions which I had been making orally for improving the PM's security management aspects. I was asked by her to send it by the special air-mail bag of the Calcutta office of the Subsidiary Intelligence Bureau as early as possible.

This was done by me on 26th December to the best of my ability and after consulting all my VIP security colleagues in Calcutta. I learnt later, through Grewal, that the Prime Minister had duly appreciated the points painstakingly and meticulously brought out in my Note and that some of these were in the process of implementation. One 'visible' outcome was the creation of a new post of PM's Security Co-ordinator, which, I learnt later, was taken over by someone, an IAS officer, who never had the exposure to this kind of sensitive task. Incidentally, I had suggested two names for this critical assignment, both of whom had retired from service then but were mentally and physically in excellent condition – perhaps the best possible VIP security experts produced in our country till then which we could think of during the period - GC Dutt and John Lobo, in that order.

West Bengal Congress leaders' bizarre request

While ending this part about Rajiv Gandhi's visits to West Bengal during 1984-87, I cannot resist the temptation of narrating an episode which I had to handle as the VVIP's security officer of the State: Sonia Gandhi used to accompany Rajiv Gandhi during most of these tours and she used to sit in one of the two front seats, the other being occupied by the 'VVIP driver' himself, i.e., the PM. Whenever, the Prime Minister went up the rostrum at scheduled places of public meetings, Sonia Gandhi also was invariably escorted by the local party leaders. Generally, two or three of the important leaders of the state party also used to be part of the PM's convoy and they travelled in a separate car which was placed in the convoy, after the spare VIP car. Generally the state Congress leaders like Pranab Mukherjee (present President of India), Priya Ranjan Dasmunshi, Pradip Bhattacharjee and Subrata Mukherjee used to be part of this entourage and all of them were known to me.

These gentlemen had obviously seen the PM talking to me once in a while in his usual smiling and affable manner. This might have prompted two of them to make an unexpected and unusual request to me: Could I quietly request Sonia Gandhi to flash an occasional smile while seated on the dais or in the VIP car, especially when the VIP car was stopped or slowed down by the PM to greet the people, along the route. I was plainly taken aback by such an unusual, though understandable, request of the party leaders. My response to them was spontaneous and unequivocal, somewhat to the following effect: 'All of you know of the circumstances leading to the brutal murder of Rajivji's mother by her own security guards. His wife Soniaji knew very well that her husband too will continue to be the target of brutal terrorists and assassins and the slightest lapse on the part of the security personnel would prove to be disastrous. In a situation like this, would it not be improper and inhuman on the part of anybody to request Soniaji to put on an artificial smile? I am sorry to say that none of us should make such an outlandish request to her!'

Rajiv Gandhi's innovative steps in administration

As the new Prime Minister, Rajiv Gandhi introduced some welcome changes in administrative practices in the Government of India during 1985-86. One such step was to arrange postings at the higher levels in such a manner that the holders of top posts could have a secure tenure, but no extensions, and the successor in office was to be inducted well in advance and the names were to be made known in advance so that there was no scope for lobbying.

This principle was to apply to all senior posts in the Government of India – IAS, IPS and other Services as well. Himself being a straightforward person, Rajiv Gandhi was alien to the crooked ways of functioning and manipulative genius of a certain class of bureaucrats and politicians. Incidentally he himself realised this much later and with due honesty admitted this suo motu during a conversation which I had with him in 1991 after he ceased to be the Prime Minister. This would be narrated subsequently. In accordance with the new norms for postings, I was inducted into the Central Bureau of Investigation (CBI) as Additional Director. The scheme was somewhat as follows as I could learn after joining the CBI in September, 1987: the incumbent Director CBI, MG Katre, was due for retirement in October, 1987 and was to be succeeded by CM Radhakrishnan Nair who was meanwhile promoted as Special Director for the interim period, and I was to succeed Nair since he was to have a stint for hardly one year.

It is a different matter, however, that Katre, under the pretext of investigation of the Bofors case, could get three extensions and continued as Director, CBI till October, 1989, completely ruling out any possibility of Nair becoming the Director. Meanwhile, the Bofors episode had started unravelling disturbing facets which were being exploited fully by two classes of people. The first category consisted of the usual 'power brokers', a class which was earlier castigated rightly by Rajiv Gandhi himself while he was the General Secretary of his party. But the force of circumstances made him succumb to this façade of protective ring ('*chakra vyuha*') of some persons belonging to this category, civil servants and others. The other category was composed of the political class with vested interests, who knew that unless the image of this dynamic and forward-looking young PM was effectively demolished, they stood no chance of achieving their political ambitions in the foreseeable future!

Rajiv Gandhi's humane gesture

Rajiv Gandhi thanked us for bringing these grim facts to his notice for the first time and immediately rang up the Home Minister to say that all our recommendations were to be complied with during the next 30 days!

Another episode calls for recapitulation since it reveals Rajiv Gandhi's capacity to take quick and totally objective decisions even when there were likely traces of emotional involvement, as some had wrongly attributed to him. The Union Home Ministry had constituted perhaps during 1986-87 a 'high-powered committee' headed by the Director/Addl Director, CBI to monitor all cases in Punjab and elsewhere arising out of the Khalistani Terrorist Acts. The DGPs of Punjab, Haryana, UP, Madhya Pradesh, Maharashtra, Andhra Pradesh and few other states were the members along with a senior representative each from the MHA and the Intelligence Bureau and the Commissioner of Delhi Police. Quarterly meetings of the Committee used to be held in the CBI office at CGO Complex, New Delhi, to monitor the progress of investigation/trial of all cases coming under the above category.

Meanwhile the CBI Director Katre was too preoccupied with and involved in the Bofors related matters. As such, it fell to my lot to chair its sessions. In course of its deliberations on June 9, 1988, I learnt that nearly three hundred persons, mostly from Punjab, were detained and kept in Jodhpur Jail (Rajasthan), commonly known as the Jodhpur detainees. On questioning some of the Punjab Police and CBI officers, I learnt that many of the detainees were old and infirm persons but further details were not readily available.

I wanted to have all possible details – the exact number of detainees, since when detained, age, ailments if any and general health condition, home address, next of kin, etc. Accordingly, a CBI team was sent to Jodhpur with due authorisation from us to collect the above particulars and also meet as many of the detainees as possible, especially the old and infirm persons. The CBI team returned after about a week and submitted its detailed report, depicting a very grim and depressing situation: there were at least one hundred detainees who were above the age of 70 years, some suffering from serious illnesses like TB, renal failure and some could not even see properly due to cataract or glaucoma. We felt that it was utterly inhuman and counter-productive to keep these and many other persons in detention any longer.

This prompted me to prepare a detailed note for the Home Minister, with copy to the Prime Minister, enclosing a copy of the report of the CBI team and recommended that

(a) all these hundred and odd persons, old and infirm, deserved to be released forthwith ;

(b) releasing them at Jodhpur (in one far off corner of Rajasthan) and expecting them to get back to their respective native places in Punjab would amount to another 'punishment' for them. Instead, they should be taken to Chandigarh in a government chartered plane, wherefrom the Punjab Government should be required to reach these persons in government or hired transport to their respective villages.

(c) The remaining detainees should be screened by a joint team of CBI and Punjab Police once every three months so that the process of their release may continue, except for those who were still considered to be posing a serious security threat.

I finally mentioned in my Note that if the above steps were taken urgently, there would not only be a considerable lessening in the level of alienation among the Sikhs but also a positive surge of goodwill among the common people of Punjab and elsewhere among the Sikh community in general. I personally took my Note and all connected papers to the Home Minister Sardar Buta Singh. The suave and soft-spoken Sardarji thanked me and the CBI team for our painstaking report and also agreed with my suggestions. However, he desired that I should show all these papers to the Prime Minister personally, for which he arranged an appointment for me with the latter. When I met Rajiv Gandhi on the date and time indicated by him, I was not surprised at his response. Apart from thanking us for bringing these grim facts to his notice for the first time, he immediately rang up the Home Minister to say that all our recommendations were to be complied with during the next 30 days! And that were complied with.

Unforgettable 'coffee meeting' with Rajiv Gandhi

It came as a total surprise to me in mid-June, 1989 when I was asked by the PS to PM Vincent George for an informal 'coffee' meeting with the Prime Minister at his residence on June 19, 1989 at 09.30 am, with no indication of the subject matter for discussion. As I was ushered into his drawing room, I saw a radiant and relaxed Rajiv Gandhi, just as I was used to observing him in course of his visits to West Bengal during 1984-87.

After having ordered some snacks and coffee for the two of us, he started off by saying that he still remembered his visits to West Bengal, mostly accompanied by his wife, and the meticulous care which we took during his hectic tours. He then enquired whether I was happy to be back in Delhi and in the CBI; I answered in the affirmative and thanked him for having selected me for re-induction into CBI.

At this stage, I also mentioned that as desired by him, perhaps during 1986-87, the draft of a proposed CBI Act in place of the complicated and somewhat outdated Delhi Special Police Establishment Act of 1946, which governed the functioning of the CBI and it still does, and that such a draft had been prepared by a team of competent CBI officers during the past two years, with due consultation with its senior Law Officers including its Legal Advisor. Sometime after joining the CBI as its Additional Director, I was required to give the finishing touches at the final stage which I had done by then. However, I submitted that considerable care and caution had been given to the matter by all concerned in the CBI during the past two years. While drafting the law, the focus of our combined efforts had been to ensure that an institution of national importance like the CBI should never be allowed to be misused for extraneous considerations either by any CBI functionaries or by any government for all time to come.

Secondly, I submitted to the Prime Minister that though the draft legislation has introduced at the specific suggestion of the PMO and/or Chidambaram, then MOS incharge of the CBI on behalf of the PM, the concept of 'federal offences' along with some related provisions thereon, e.g., the appropriate machinery for investigation of the federal offences and reasons thereof, etc. I further submitted that I had some reservations regarding the concept of 'federal offences' because it may work like a double-edged weapon. This apart, one can reasonably expect serious reservations from most states in vesting additional police/investigating powers at the central level unless they are assured of some institutional mechanism whereby any possible misuse by the CBI itself or by the Central Government through the CBI could be precluded and this too needed to be built into the Act. Even the suspicion of misuse by the CBI would damage the continuing credibility of the organisation. During the above submissions by me, the PM at times put some probing questions for seeking further clarifications on the above points but he did not try to overrule my view-points. On the contrary, I had the impression that he substantially agreed with my submissions.

I took leave of him, after thanking him for calling me and also for allowing me to express my views candidly. As I was moving towards the exit door, he suddenly spoke out thus: "Mr Mukherjee, let me tell you that I have full faith in you" ! Such a pleasant and unexpected gesture on his part was a surprise and I retraced my steps back to him and said "Sir, I am indeed grateful for this kind gesture on your part. Kindly allow me to say that as a proud professional, I take it for granted that I enjoy my PM's trust. However, if at any stage I feel that I enjoy less than your fullest confidence, I would be the first person to come and tell you, 'Sir, here are my papers and kindly allow me to go home!' He burst out laughing and called me back for another round of coffee"!

As I sat down again, he asked for some more coffee for us and started recalling some of the interesting but funny episodes during his long pre-election and election tours in West Bengal and elsewhere during 1986-87 and thereafter. I was pleasantly surprised that he still remembered the role (a small one though !) played by me during 1987 in bringing together the West Bengal Chief Minister Jyoti Basu, Subash Ghising and the Prime Minister together for the first time at Darjeeling Raj Bhavan as the first step in bringing about the subsequent rapprochement in the turbulent GNLF agitation. He also mentioned about the utmost care and caution which I and my officers used to take along with the SPG team for ensuring the fullest possible safety and security for him as well as for his wife who used to accompany him during most of his visits to West Bengal.

Bofors Gun Deal: *Rajiv's Candid Revelation*

> *Rajiv Gandhi came to know that some senior officers of the armed forces had been surreptitiously collecting huge amounts of money as 'commissions' in most of the major defence purchases, quite often in connivance with some ministers, middlemen and civilian officers... He discussed this problem with some of his trusted colleagues and advisers to devise alternative measures which would largely prevent the nexus between officers of the armed forces, middlemen, ministers and bureaucrats... But the wild, motivated and adverse publicity on the Bofors issue frustrated the prospect of proceeding further in this matter...*

I still do not know what 'possessed' me at this stage, during the second round of coffee, to put across to Rajiv Gandhi the 'most audacious and atrocious query' which I did in total disregard of propriety and risking my entire career. Anybody would have considered it impudent and impertinent, to say the least. Suddenly, and somewhat impulsively, I uttered: "Sir, before I came over to Delhi to join the CBI in 1987, I saw some media reports to the effect that you made a statement in Parliament, perhaps in the context of the Bofors debate, to the effect that 'Neither I nor any member of my family had taken even a single rupee ...', adding that the little that I had seen and known about him, it was atrocious on the part of any person with the slightest regard for truth and a modicum of political honesty to suggest anything to the contrary. It saddened me that our Prime Minister had to make such a statement at all…!"

Soon after blurting it out, I prepared myself for a stern rebuke and a thorough dressing down. Instead, what he said in an unbelievably calm and composed manner came as a great surprise, immeasurably adding to my respect and faith in our young Prime Minister. In quite a matter of fact manner, he reminded me about some of his earlier statements as the leader of the Youth Wing and later as the General Secretary of his party about the unholy nexus between some of their party functionaries surreptitiously collecting funds from industrial and business houses in the name of the party, perhaps only a part of which was deposited to the party and the unaccounted rest pocketed by them.

"Mr. Mukherjee, you may perhaps imagine that a big all-India party like ours does need substantial amounts of money just for its routine administration throughout the year. This requirement assumes a huge proportion on the eve of Assembly and/or Parliamentary elections. This leads to massive fund collections by important party functionaries all over the country, which leads to an almost unbreakable unholy quid pro quo nexus between unscrupulous party functionaries, ministers and businessmen. I could sense this as the party's General Secretary or even as its youth leader earlier when I had to enter the political arena with considerable reluctance…".

Sensing that, for whatever reasons, he was in a reminiscent mood, I sat quietly without disrupting his train of thoughts. What he stated thereafter candidly can only be summarised as I am not in a position to quote his exact words at this distant past of nearly 24 years: After becoming the Prime Minister towards the end of

1984, he came to know that some senior officers of the armed forces had been surreptitiously collecting huge amounts of money as 'commissions' in respect of most of the defence purchases, quite often in connivance with some ministers, middlemen and civilian officers as well. Though it was in public knowledge for long, no serious or systematic attempt was made to put a stop to such a continuing malady.

He discussed this problem with some of his trusted colleagues and advisers when it was suggested by some that all commissions as payable or usually paid to middlemen should be banned but the commissions to be given as a matter of routine practice by the suppliers of major defence materials could be pooled under the care of some non-government entity which could be utilised solely for the purpose of meeting the inescapable expenses of the party. As Rajiv Gandhi further stated, such a step would largely prevent the collusive nexus between the middlemen, ministers, bureaucrats and that such a step could enable the Government to do away with the quid pro quo relationship with some unscrupulous businessmen and equally unscrupulous politicians and bureaucrats.

Hence, he endorsed the same. He also indicated that he favoured some legislation in line with the practices of some of the western countries where contributions to party funds by business and industrial houses and individuals were allowed with provisions for their proper accounting, auditing and public disclosure. But the wild, motivated and widespread adverse publicity obscured the prospect of proceeding further in the above manner. I had no reason to doubt that he was speaking straight from the heart, and perhaps waiting to unburden himself to a minor cog like me in the governmental wheel but trusting in my sense of judgement and discretion. I could just manage to mumble a few words of thanks and gratitude for the trust reposed in me and quietly left the room.

Later, in retrospect, I surmised that Rajiv Gandhi knew that I had been inducted into CBI as Addl Director for my eventual taking over as its Director when Katre (IPS/1952/Maharashtra) was to retire in October, 1987 and his successor, Radhakrishnan Nair /1954, was also to retire by the end of 1988. However, taking advantage of the Bofors imbroglio, Katre could get two or three successive extensions and thereby ruling out any possibility of Nair, an outstanding officer steeped in CBI tradition and its professional culture, reaching the CBI's top slot. By implication, the above developments also cut into the period which I would have had as the CBI chief in the normal course.

I looked at it philosophically and never allowed my professionalism or peace of mind to be distorted or disturbed. Perhaps Rajiv Gandhi being an extremely sensitive person, might have felt unhappy at such turn of events, cutting short the prospects of Nair and me at the fag end of our career. I guess, my coffee invitation was his way of saying 'I am sorry for the unforeseen turn of events'. And what a gracious way of doing so, especially when he as the Prime Minister was not obliged to do so!

But more than the above, it dawned on me that what transpired that day between the two of us towards the end of the 'coffee meeting' could not have been thought out by him in advance when I was invited to his presence. All that he mentioned to me, almost like a soliloquy and with childlike simplicity, could not have but a deeply moving impact on me, knowing what he had to endure during the previous couple of years. I also felt that sharing this episode with others then would have amounted to betraying his trust, which I could never even think of doing. However, at this distant time and that too long after his tragic death, I owe it to posterity to narrate the full and complete disclosure of all that transpired between the two of us during this memorable 'coffee meeting' with this remarkable human being whose trust I was privileged to receive in ample measure.

Eventually on October 31, 1989 I took over charge from Katre as Director, CBI, Nair having retired from the service earlier. On 25th November, I had to leave Delhi as head of the Indian delegation to the Interpol General Assembly Session in its new location at Lyon, France where the Interpol's new HQ was shifted from an odd location in Paris and was to be inaugurated by the French President Francois Mitteraund.

By the time I returned to Delhi in the early morning of December 3, 1989 a sea change had taken place in India's political arena brought about by the Lok Sabha elections, replacing the Congress led by Rajiv Gandhi and bringing in the Janata Dal led by VP Singh. The new Government of National Front was sworn in on 5th December with VP Singh as the Prime Minister and Chaudhary Devi Lal as the Deputy PM.

As an unfortunate legacy of our politico-administrative culture, quite a few heads of top bureaucratic echelons in the government started rolling from about mid-December - Cabinet Secretary, Home, Revenue and Defence Secretaries and inevitably, of course, the CBI and the IB Directors, among some others. I was 'kicked upstairs' in January, 1990 as the Special Secretary in the

Ministry of Home Affairs. Though there was some media outcry against my ouster from CBI, I took it in my stride and enjoyed the respite from CBI's daunting schedule, which gave me sometime to catch up on studies of my interest.

Prelude to my return to West Bengal: 'The Eagle has Landed!'

> *As I entered New Delhi's Banga Bhavan on an invitation from the West Bengal Chief Minister Jyoti Basu, I was taken aback when the venerable Benoy Chaudhury just said softly "Don't say "no" to the Chief Minister!*

During my tenure as MHA's Special Secretary in 1990, I learnt informally that the West Bengal Government was facing considerable public resentment against police functioning there, with episodes like Bantala where two or three respectable women officers were brutally assaulted while returning to Calcutta from an inspection tour, gang rape of some women, perhaps in the district of 24 Parganas close to Calcutta, leading to heightened public outcry against the government in general and the police in particular.

On top of these, I was told, Jyoti Basu was peeved at my ouster from the post of Director, CBI by their 'friendly government' at the Centre led by VP Singh. The cumulative effect of all these might have prompted him to ask the then Chief Secretary and my old friend from the University days, Tarun Dutt to persuade me to return to West Bengal, which I politely spurned, perhaps three times within the course of as many months. At that time, Jyoti Basu's all-India stature and respectability was well-known. Hence, all that was needed for him was to speak to the Prime Minister himself and ask for my repatriation back to the state and nobody would have dared to spurn him!

Jyoti Basu's innate civility and administrative propriety

What I state now would reveal, if such a revelation is at all called for, Jyoti Basu's innate civility and administrative propriety even while he was at the zenith of his power and authority. On coming to know of my reluctance to come back to West Bengal at that stage, he simply asked the Chief Secretary to leave the file with him. A few days later I received a telephone call from his Personal Secretary, wanting to know if I would be in Delhi on a certain date for a meeting with the Chief Minister, though he did not know what was the meeting about. The Chief Minister had been coming to Delhi almost once or twice every month for official engagements as also for attending the Politbureau or Central Committee meetings of the CPM.

The day prior to the date of the scheduled meeting with him in New Delhi's Banga Bhavan 3, Hailey Road, off Kasturba Gandhi Marg, one officer in his personal staff informed me about the time and the venue of the meeting. As I arrived there a few minutes in advance, I found Benoy Babu, late Benoy Chaudury, the senior most member in West Bengal Cabinet, next only to the Chief Minister, having his usual stroll along the corridor. As I greeted him before being ushered into Room no. 109 where the Chief Minister was already present, I was taken aback when the venerable Benoy Babu just said softly "Don't say 'no' to the CM"! After I entered Chief Minister's room and greeted him, for the next 15 minutes or so he spoke to me about some of the current problems being faced by him in West Bengal, not all related to police matters, enquired about my wife and our two sons and so on. Then suddenly he came to the main issue of my going back to West Bengal as Director General of Police (DGP) and stated that I need not have any reservations and that all my suggestions for improvement of the police in West Bengal would be taken care of by him and also my friend, the Chief Secretary. Before I could respond to him, he called for the Chief Secretary who was in one of the adjacent rooms.

As Tarun Das came in, the Chief Minister straight away asked him to immediately get in touch with the Cabinet Secretary Vinod Pande so that an early order could be issued by them for my release and repatriation to West Bengal, – 'with full protection of my present rank (Secretary to the Government of India) and pay'. Perhaps I happened to be the first Director General of Police in any state then with the rank and pay of the Chief Secretary, not a big deal though for me. It speaks volumes about Jyoti Basu's human touch, besides his ability to take quick decisions.

So I landed up at Calcutta, took charge as the state's DGP with effect from the afternoon of 31st August, 1990 and got involved in the usual hectic schedule. It did not take me long to transmit the required signals to all concerned that sloth and lack of integrity, at whatever level, will neither be countenanced nor go unpunished. As one journalist jocularly mentioned 'the eagle has landed!'

At the very early stage, it was made clear by me to all concerned, including the ministers and others, that the professional hierarchy and chain of command in a basically uniformed organisation like the police should not be breached. Our officers were also specially instructed not to entertain or encourage political intervention in the discharge of their lawfully enjoined duties. Any undue pressure or threat from any such quarters was to be brought directly to my notice over phone and it was then my duty to protect them against any such brandishment or allurement.

There were three or four instances where I had to intervene with ministers or other powerful political personalities to put a stop to such attempts at interference either in the matter of transfers and postings of policemen of various ranks or on matters pertaining to filing of FIRs and investigation of criminal cases. I must admit, however, that most of them including our officers down to police station level rose to the occasion and gave me unstinting support in my endeavours to restore or maintain professional functioning of the police. To cap it all, the Chief Minister as also the Chief Secretary and the Home Secretary were never found wanting in extending their support to all such endeavours of ours.

Rajiv's offer of Prime Ministership to Jyoti Basu

> *...All the implications and finer points made out by me in favour of Jyoti Basu accepting Rajiv Gandhi's offer of Prime Ministership, though presumably for a short period of 8-12 months, went over the heads of the Left Front leaders – thanks to their blinkered vision!*

Once during my stint as the Home Ministry's Special Secretary, I came to know through a personal friend, Pandit NK Sharma, that Rajiv Gandhi may take certain steps to ease out VP Singh as the Prime Minister and that Jyoti Basu's name figured in Rajiv Gandhi's list of three prospective PMs who may be supported by Rajiv

Gandhi. I was informally requested to persuade Mr Basu to agree to this suggestion. This I did, first by sounding him out but his response was that he was not in a position to express any view and that decisions on such matters were to be taken by their party's Central Committee and Politbureau.

Additionally, I was asked by the CM to speak to some of their senior party leaders about any such proposal. Thereafter I did speak to some of the important leaders in both CPM and the Left Front, making it clear that I had no personal interest in the matter except to suggest that such an eventuality, though fragile and may be for a short duration of 8-12 months, it would be in the larger national interest as well as the long-term interest of West Bengal: at least for some months the Chief Minister and other ministers of West Bengal would not be required to go to Delhi almost every month with a 'beggars' bowl' for obtaining the Centre's approval for so many of its important projects; secondly, and hopefully, Jyoti Basu would be able to leave his imprint as an administrator with civility, straightforward dealings and statesmanlike qualities in managing the country's governance–traits which the country will appreciate for a long time to come. Unfortunately, all my exertions proved futile - thanks to the blinkered views of most of the Left Front leaders!

Ultimately Chandrasekhar, (the last name in Rajiv Gandhi's list - after Devi Lal and Jyoti Basu), became the Prime Minister on November 10, 1990. He was known to be an astute politician and an effective speaker in Parliament. Unfortunately, it was also public knowledge that he did not enjoy a good reputation in regard to his integrity. His so called ashram at Bhondsi in Haryana on Delhi-Haryana border was a sprawling farmhouse as also the known centre of intrigues and dubious deals!

Rajiv Gandhi's second offer of PM to Jyoti Basu

It was generally known that Chandrasekhar's Prime Ministership was a stop-gap arrangement and that efforts were set afoot again to persuade Jyoti Basu to accept Rajiv Gandhi's offer of Prime Ministership. By that time I had gone back to West Bengal as DGP since 1st September, 1990. One of Rajiv Gandhi's trusted emissary of that period, who knew me personally, Pandit NK Sharma[7], conveyed to me Rajiv Gandhi's message over phone – to try once again to persuade Jyoti Basu so that Chandrasekhar could be replaced by a person of Jyoti Basu's eminence and reputation. I reminded him about my previous effort and Jyoti Basu's response thereto and also stated that it would be impudent on my part to expect Jyoti Basu to change his mind because they were 'basically strong political beings', with full knowledge that he would be PM, if at all, for a brief period of 8-12 months.

I did not know that during my above conversation with his emissary, Rajiv Gandhi was on the extension line of the telephone. At this stage Rajiv Gandhi came directly on the line and asked me what would I suggest so as to be able to put across his proposal to Jyoti Basuji more forcefully. Quite impromptu, and without any authority from any quarters, I just mentioned two minimum preconditions on the basis of which I may do my best to broach his proposal to Jyoti Basu again: first, Jyoti Basu should be fully assured by him (Rajiv Gandhi) personally that he would have at least a minimum tenure of one year as the PM; secondly, when eventually the Lok Sabha elections are decided upon, the Congress should agree to concede a certain number of seats in various states to the Left Front because they were basically strong 'political beings'. Surprisingly, after questioning me on some points arising out of the aforesaid views of mine, Rajiv Gandhi virtually agreed to both the propositions, so wildly and blindly put across by me in my naivete. He then wanted me to give some rough indication of sharing the next Lok Sabha seats between the Congress and the Left Front. At that time I had some idea about the number of LS seats held by the LF parties in various states.

Once again, in my naivete, I gave him a rough idea about the number of seats which may be offered to the LF – 20 each in UP and Bihar, 5 each in Punjab and Haryana, and 10 each in Maharashtra, Madhya Pradesh, Andhra Pradesh, Orissa, Tamil Nadu and Karnataka and so on. I knew that even if that many seats were conceded, the Left Front would find it difficult to put up their candidates for so many seats in most of those states. After some questioning, and to my surprise, Rajiv Gandhi agreed to such a proposition and asked me to repeat the number of seats and the states for which these may have to be conceded, noted them down and read out to me.

I also suggested that the above two propositions should be conveyed on his behalf by his emissary and later to be confirmed by him personally to Mr Basu and that his emissary should come down to Calcutta for follow-up talks on his behalf with Jyoti Basu and other Left Front leaders as may be necessary. I agreed to fix for his emissary appointments with Jyoti Basu and others for this discussion.

The emissary did come to Calcutta on the third day or so, by which time I could persuade Jyoti Basu to meet this gentleman and discuss this sensitive matter directly with this emissary of Rajiv Gandhi. The emissary insisted that I should accompany him for this meeting with Jyoti Basu.

After the gentleman had put across the two propositions from Rajiv Gandhi, Jyoti Basu's response was as I had predicted that in the light of their party discipline, he was not in a position to express his personal reactions and that such matters are decided by the party and advised the emissary to put across Rajiv Gandhi's propositions to some of the important party leaders of the state who, in turn, would take it up with their central leadership, if they considered it necessary.

Such meetings did take place. However, it appeared to me that the party leaders with whom the discussion took place in the house of Biplab Dasgupta, an eminent scholar who belonged to the CPM, totally failed to appreciate the long-term implications for the state and the country as a whole. Though I was a mere spectator except to explain to them in Bengali where necessary, my worst conjecture proved right - all the implications and finer points went over their heads. Thus ended the second opportunity of putting up the Left Front's best foot forward in the larger interest of West Bengal by having a person of Jyoti Basu's stature as the country's Prime Minister, even for a short period of 8-12 months!

CPM's Himalayan Blunders - Twice over!

In 1996, with the fall of the 13 day old Vajpayee Government and despite the consent of the prominent leaders of the United Front to get Jyoti Basu to head their Government in Delhi, this prospect too was shot down by the CPM Central Committee/Politbureau through a 'majority view' ! Some years later, Jyoti Basu termed it as his party's Himalayan blunder'. However, it is not generally known that such blunders had taken place twice during 1990-91 itself as narrated by me earlier, largely because of the unrealistic, short-sighted and 'blunder-proof' mindset of the CPM leaders. Like me, I know of many others who felt that the very complexion of the murky political and administrative ethos had a fair chance of healthy transformation with Jyoti Basu at the apex of governance of the country.

My last meeting with Rajiv Gandhi

> *Mr Mukherjee, you may perhaps know by now that we will win this election and we will come back.... I would insist on your coming back to Delhi then to assist me in a number of ways...*

One of the annual rituals of the police in India has been the yearly Conference of the DGPs of states, traditionally hosted by the Director, IB. The 1991 Conference took place from 19th to 22nd March. After attending this Conference, I was to return to Calcutta by the morning flight next day since I was scheduled to attend an important meeting there the same afternoon. As was my old habit, I preferred to stay at Banga Bhavan in one of the modest first floor rooms overlooking the Hailey Road, New Delhi.

On the late evening of March 22, 1991, I unexpectedly received a telephone call from a gentleman whom I had known for some years, my old friend NK Sharma *alias* Panditji. He mentioned that Rajiv Gandhi had come to know that I was in Delhi and that he was very keen that I must have coffee with him next morning before I returned to Calcutta. I told my friend that even though Rajivji was no longer the PM, I had the same respect and regard for him as I had earlier and that I had to return to Calcutta by the next day's morning flight because of an important meeting scheduled there, adding that in the near future I would visit Delhi specially to call on Rajivji. At this stage, the gentleman asked me to speak to Rajivji who was on the line. Till then I did not know that my friend was with Rajivji at his 10, Janpath residence. Obviously, Rajiv Gandhi was on a parallel line and had followed the entire conversation between me and my friend.

Rajiv Gandhi came straight to the point: "Mr Mukherjee, can I suggest something? If you ask your Banga Bhavan people to go to the airport a little in advance, they can book your baggage, get the boarding pass and wait for you there. I will send some gentleman in one of our security-vetted cars to pick you up from Banga Bhavan around 8 in the morning and bring you straight to our residence so that no time is lost in security checking, etc. Then we could have some coffee together and talk for sometime and the same car and the gentleman concerned would take you to the departure wing of the airport in good time for you to board the Calcutta-bound plane".

I could just thank him for taking such a lot of trouble and say "Sir, I will go by the 'drill' laid down by you!" Thus I was destined to meet him as scheduled by him. I would have regretted for the rest of life if I failed to meet him this time. I had a hunch that perhaps he wanted to discuss and tell me something of significance, or else why should he waste his time on me in the midst of his known hectic schedule–the Lok Sabha Election process was almost half way through and obviously he had been holding election meetings all over the country.

My friend NK Sharma escorted me from Banga Bhavan in one of the security-vetted cars of Rajiv Gandhi, ushered me directly to Rajiv Gandhi's drawing room via Vincent George's chamber. When I greeted him, I saw the same beaming and smiling face as ever and he made me sit by his side on a sofa. After a couple of minutes of exchange of pleasantries and while sipping coffee, what he stated during the next 15-20 minutes can perhaps be summarised thus: "Mr. Mukherjee, you were one of the few persons who used to speak to me, especially during 1985-89, without any reservations and also without any 'hidden agenda' or for advancing your personal interests but solely to safeguard my and my family's security as also to strengthen our administration. I realised only later, after ceasing to be the Prime Minister, that though most of the gentlemen whom I trusted were of impeccable character but unfortunately quite a few had been exploiting my position to further their personal interests".

What Rajiv Gandhi stated thereafter took me somewhat by surprise and I could not initially make out why he did so to me of all persons who never tried to ingratiate himself to his Prime Minister at any stage; on the contrary, I was rather blunt and 'undiplomatic' in telling him more than once during his visits to West Bengal (1985-87) that he was violating quite a few security protocols and thereby adding to our genuine worry and anxiety about the Prime Minister's and his accompanying wife's safety and security.

Rajivji reminded me about one of my remarks to him about the widespread canard against him about the Bofors' pay-off; he was obviously referring to my 'coffee meeting' with him on 19th June, 1989: "Mr Mukherjee, let me tell you something which I haven't done so far..." True to his generosity and innate qualities of a perfect gentleman, he did not specifically mention any names of the persons of either category but some of the episodes which he very briefly narrated made clear to me who these persons were–some in the IAS and the IFS, one or two in the IPS and a few who did not belong to the above categories. Some of the episodes were then known to me while the others came as a revelation. But, whatever he narrated, he did so without the slightest tinge of rancour or bitterness.

Rajiv Gandhi finally summed up by saying something to the following effect which I vividly recall even now: "Mr Mukherjee, you may perhaps know by now that we will win this election and we will come back. I wanted to tell you that I would insist on your coming back to Delhi then to assist me in a number of ways which I need not relate now. But I just wanted you to be mentally prepared for another shift to Delhi and be in good cheer and good health till then". I too wished him all the best in the years to come and also be in the best of health and happiness in the midst of the hectic election campaign by him. It was palpably apparent to me that he had considerably matured during the past year or so after having reflected deeply on ceasing to be the Prime Minister. As I took leave of him, he made another of his generous gestures by seeing me off up to the exit door. I could never imagine then that I will never have the opportunity of meeting again this wonderful gentleman!

Six weeks after this meeting, what happened at Sriperumbudur, Tamil Nadu, has remained till this day as the most tragic and shocking event for me personally as also for the country as a whole. I still feel that the very character of our country's politics and administration, nay the whole gamut of culture of governance would have assumed a decisively modern and vibrant character under a more mature Rajiv Gandhi in his second innings of prime ministership. In spite of his political differences with the Congress, Rajiv Gandhi's brutal assassination was strongly condemned by Jyoti Basu as the "most heinous, frightening and utterly condemnable act which tragically cut short the young political leader's life" and that this tragic episode has "shocked the entire nation". And I knew that Jyoti Basu meant every word of it from the bottom of his heart.

For a very long time after Rajiv Gandhi's assassination, and even now, I cannot reconcile myself to quite a few of the serious lapses on the part of some of the political leaders and officers who were known to be close to Rajiv Gandhi. Thus, firstly, even a 'semi-literate' person in the craft of intelligence and VIP protection could not have been so naïve as to be almost oblivious to the fact that India's role in helping Sri Lankan Government on the emotive issue of LTTE-Sri Lankan Government conflict, Rajiv Gandhi was bound to be a specially marked man for the fanatical and well-organised terrorist outfit of the LTTE, and that such a threat did not evaporate even when he ceased to be the Prime Minister. On the contrary, his security was bound to be threatened manifold as soon as the SPG security cover was withdrawn on the specious plea that the SPG was meant only for the incumbent Prime Minister! Wasn't the rule changed shortly after Rajiv's assassination to provide SPG cover to all kinds of persons and a host of their family members as well–some with even dubious reputation?

The highest or the lower levels of security cover by the SPG or otherwise continues to be provided on the basis of the 'threat perception', prepared by a group of security experts in the Intelligence Bureau, in respect of the person concerned. Even a person with a modest expertise in security matters should have known that the threat perception for Rajiv Gandhi and his family members was of the same level, if not much higher, whether he continued to be the PM or not. It could, at most, be a small and silly technicality regarding the rules/law governing the SPG deployment. Even this silly technical point could be easily taken care of by allowing the same set of SPG personnel to continue with the task of providing the needed security cover, not necessarily as 'SPG personnel' but under some other nomenclature and this could have continued till the law was changed, as was done but only after the terrible damage had been perpetrated! This serious gap and even more serious lapse was promptly seized upon by the cruel and treacherous LTTE leadership.

Rajiv Gandhi assassination case

On May 21, 1991, former Prime Minister Rajiv Gandhi was assassinated at Sriperumbudur near Chennai by a suicide bomber, Dhanu, of the Liberation Tigers of Tamil Eelam (LTTE). This dastardly act was meticulously planned and executed, which shocked the entire nation. Investigation of this case was assigned to the CBI's Special Investigation Team (SIT) under the charge of an IG-level officer, DR Karthikeyan. After a meticulous investigation, the SIT came to the conclusion that the LTTE was behind the assassination and submitted to the designated court a chargesheet against 41 persons. Of the 41 accused, three were absconding and could not be tried.

They were LTTE chief V Prabhakaran, its intelligence wing chief Pottu Amman, and the deputy chief of the LTTE women's intelligence wing, Akila. Twelve among the 41 died meanwhile, and so the charges against them abated. The remaining 26 stood trial in the designated court at Poonamallee near Chennai.

In his judgement delivered on January 28, 1998, the designated judge V Navaneetham pronounced all 26 guilty of murder (Section 302 of the Indian Penal Code/ IPC, read with Section 120-B, IPC i.e. Criminal Conspiracy to commit murder) as also under some provisions of the Terrorist and Disruptive Activities (Prevention) Act / TADA.

The charge against Prabhakaran was that he ordered the assassination. Pottu Amman conspired with Prabhakaran to carry it out. The charge against Akila was that she, in tandem with them, planned the assassination and arranged for its execution. Dhanu, an LTTE cadre, was to carry out the assassination along with Subha. Sivarasan, LTTE intelligence wing member, led the nine-member assassination squad, which reached Kodiakkarai in Tamil Nadu from the Jaffna peninsula on May 1. Sivarasan and Subha committed suicide at Konankunte near Bangalore on August 19, 1991, when they were cornered by the SIT team, aided by local police.

The chargesheet said Nalini, an Indian national and wife of Murugan, accompanied Sivarasan, Dhanu, Subha and Haribabu to the assassination site. Murugan, a Sri Lankan Tamil and LTTE intelligence wing cadre, acted as a conduit between Sivarasan and Nalini's family. Perarivalan, an Indian, helped Sivarasan and Murugan in planning and executing the conspiracy. He bought two battery cells on Sivarasan's instructions and gave them to him. These were used by Dhanu in her suicide belt. Perarivalan also bought a battery to operate an illegal wireless set, which was installed in Vijayan's (another accused in the case) house to send messages to Pottu Amman. Perarivalan bought the Kodak film used by Haribabu (photographer) to film the macabre incident.

Haribabu died in the blast that killed Rajiv Gandhi and quite a few others also lost their lives in the deadly blast.

The designated court's verdict

After the designated court awarded death sentences to all the 26 accused, they appealed in the Supreme Court. On May 11, 1999, Justices KT Thomas, DP Wadhwa and Syed Shah Mohammed Quadri confirmed the death sentences awarded to Nalini, Murugan, Santhan and Perarivalan but altered the death sentences of Robert Payas, Jayakumar and Ravichandran to life imprisonment.

However, Justice Thomas in his dissenting judgement in regard to Nalini said, "She became an obedient participant without doing dominant role. She was persistently brainwashed by A-3 (Murugan) who became her husband and then father of her child... She realised only at Sriperumbudur that Dhanu was going to kill Rajiv Gandhi. But she would not have dared to retreat from the scene because she was tucked into the tentacles of the conspiracy... She knew how Sivarasan and Santhan had liquidated those who did not stand by them..." Justice Thomas added that it could not be overlooked that she was the mother of a little girl who was born in captivity. Since the death sentence has been confirmed on the father Murugan and the child had to be saved from "imposed orphanhood," the judge said, "the sentence passed on her is altered to one of the imprisonment for life".

Of the 19 other accused, the judges absolved 18 of taking part in the conspiracy. Although the judges confirmed the sentences awarded to them by the lower court under the Arms Act, the Explosive Substances Act, the Passport Act, and so on, they were freed because they had already served out their terms. S Sanmugavadaivelu, who was charged only under TADA, was acquitted.

Nalini, Murugan, Santhan and Perarivalan filed petitions in the Sureme Court, seeking a review of the death sentences awarded to them. On October 8, 1999, Justices Thomas, Wadhwa and Quadri reconfirmed the death sentences. Justice Thomas, who gave a dissenting judgement with regard to Nalini, again said that her review petition "should be allowed and her sentence should be altered to imprisonment for life".

It may be mentioned in this context that the Tamil Nadu Governor Fathima Beevi accepted the recommendations of the Karunanidhi cabinet in April 2000 to commute the death sentence awarded to Nalini to imprisonment for life. Congress President Sonia Gandhi met President KR Naryanan and conveyed her family's view that Nalini's life should be spared: "It is my personal feeling, keeping in mind a child's need for a mother," Sonia Gandhi said. (*Frontline*, May 26, 2000).

Fathima Beevi rejected the petitions of Murugan, Santhan and Perarivalan. They have sent clemency petitions to the President on April 26, 2000. President Pratibha Patil's rejection of the petitions led to protests across Tamil Nadu. Madras High Court has, meanwhile, stayed for eight weeks the execution of all the convicts. No one really knows, as of now, when the "eight week" period would be over and what would follow thereafter, even in the most heinous, cold-blooded and meticulously planned murder of the country's former Prime Minister Rajiv Gandhi.

References

1 The/Gorkha National Liberation Front (GNLF) supremo, then leading a violent and widespread movement in the

hill areas of Darjeeling district and not even on talking terms with any of the ministers or other officers.

2 He is now the Governor of West Bengal.

3 From its inception, Ghising as the DGHC Chairman started behaving in an autocratic manner, as was his wont, and any voice of even minor dissent within the GNLF was ruthlessly suppressed by him. It was also alleged by some of his erstwhile close associates that Ghising was grossly misusing the funds and none was even allowed to have a peep into his utilisation of the substantial funds of the DGHC amounting to several crores of rupees. I was not surprised when I heard about all these improprieties because his autocratic style of functioning and an unhealthy level of megalomania were known to me for long. Though belated, the subsequent developments of 2006-08 too were not unexpected: the revolt by his former GNLF colleagues and supporters, formation of a parallel organisation called the Gorkha Jan Mukti Morcha (GJMM) under the leadership of Bimal Gurung and Roshan Giri, ouster of Subash Ghising from the DGHC and almost banning the latter's entry into the Darjeeling Hills areas!

4 From Jyoti Basu's memoir in Bengali "*Jatadur mone pare*" (As far as I recollect), 2006, p. 393.

5 According to Government of India's VVIP security protocol, i.e. the Blue Book, the car was to be driven only by a specially trained police/SPG driver.

6 A small SPG team along with me were invariably part of all such journeys, whether by copters or aircraft.

7 I would call him the Chanakya of the modern era.

Chapter 3

Indrajit Gupta

Who is Indrajit Gupta? Those well-versed with the Indian political landscape won't take a second to answer this query. Nevertheless it may be in order to place Indrajit Gupta in proper perspective. He was born on March 18, 1919 in Calcutta, (1, Dover Road, South Calcutta), did his schooling in Calcutta and Shimla where his ICS father SC Gupta happened to be posted. After completing his schooling, Indrajit Gupta did his graduation from Delhi's St Stephen's College and was sent to England, Cambridge University, with the hope that he would come back to India as a pucca ICS officer like quite a few others in the family including his elder brother Ranjit Gupta.[1]

Belying the expectations of his family and friends, Indrajit Gupta alias Sunny, returned to Calcutta during 1940-41 as a deeply committed Communist along with some of his friends and associates in UK like Jyoti Basu, Bhupesh Gupta, Nikhil and Renu Chakravarty, Mohan

Kumarmangalam, all of whom had come under the spell of Rajani Palme Dutt and other top leaders of the Communist Party of Great Britain as also of the eminent left-leaning academician Prof Harold Laski. By 1942-43 he had become a member of the undivided Communist Party of India and had been assigned the task of organising the workers of jute and textile mills in and around Calcutta as also of the engineering, port and dock workers of Calcutta. In due course, he became a front-ranking leader of the All India Trade Union Congress (AITUC) and quite a few of the international labour organisations as well.

His entry into the parliamentary arena started when he was elected as a member of the undivided CPI to the Lok Sabha in the 1960 by-election to the Calcutta South-West Constituency. Thereafter, there was no looking back, and Indrajit Gupta won a record 11 consecutive Lok Sabha elections in his 38-year long parliamentary career till his death in 2001. Hence, it was no surprise that this legendary parliamentarian was nominated by the successive Presidents of India as the pro tem Speaker for administering the oath of office to MPs in new Lok Sabhas for a record number of times. In 1992 Indrajit Gupta was unanimously adjudged as the 'Best Parliamentarian' and in the 1999 Joint Session of Parliament, he was bestowed the unprecedented honour of the 'Father of the House'.

My first introduction to Indrajit Gupta

> *Frankly speaking, Mr Mukherjee, I am not enamoured of the prospect of becoming Home Minister but the decision (of the United Front) stands as of now... I think you know perhaps better than me that this ministry is a complicated affair. Hence, I am requesting you to give me some briefing about the working of this ministry as also its pitfalls...*

I retired from the Indian Police Service on 1st January, 1992, thereafter I served as the Vigilance Commissioner of West Bengal around the middle of 1995. Till then, this post was considered he preserve of retired ICS/IAS officers or retired Chief Justice/Judge of the Calcutta High Court. Meanwhile, after retirement from the IPS and before joining the Vigilance Commission, I enjoyed constructing, literally brick-by-brick, our modest house 'PALASH' in Salt Lake City, almost mid-way between the City of Calcutta and its airport at Dum Dum. I had just started indulging in my old love of trees and plants, many of which were planted by me in front of our house and within our small compound. I was also trying to catch up with some readings on subjects of my interest.

Around this time, on 6th of June, 1996, I received a surprise telephone call from an entirely unexpected quarter to the following effect: "Mr Mukherjee, I am speaking from our modest, ancestral house at 1, Dover Road in the Ballygunge area of South Calcutta. You may not know me; my name is Indrajit Gupta and I happen to be an MP for some years. I need your advice and assistance in certain matters and that is why I am troubling you...".

Let me confess that I was touched by the modesty and humility of this giant of a parliamentarian whom I had never met till then but surely I could not be so ignorant as not to have heard his name or to have some idea about his widely acknowledged reputation. I replied by stating that though I had no opportunity of meeting him so far, surely I am not so ignorant as not to know at least something about him and enquired in what respect I could be of any help to him.

He briefly mentioned about formation of the new United Front Government in Delhi with Deve Gowda as Prime Minister and that his party (CPI) had decided to join the Government and that the newly-formed Government wanted him to join as its Home Minister. "Frankly speaking, Mr Mukherjee," he continued, "I am not enamoured of the prospect but the decision stands as of now. I understand that you had been in Delhi for a number of years including your stint in the CBI and the Home Ministry as its Special Secretary and as such you would know perhaps better than me that this Ministry is a complicated affair. Hence, I am requesting you to give me some briefing about the working of this ministry as also its pitfalls..."

It was mutually agreed that I would meet him in his house the next day, which I did. I informed him that I was somewhat out of touch with Delhi and the Home Ministry and as such, in addition to whatever I may be capable of sharing with him my knowledge about the MHA and its working, he may consider being briefed in greater depth and details from some of the officers in the Home Ministry then. Hence, I mentioned to him the names of some of my friends in the IAS and IPS in Delhi who were still in service or had retired only recently.

The general internal security scenario of the country, the situation in Jammu and Kashmir and the problems in the north-east states then figured in our discussion. Additionally, I gave him my personal views as to where our successive governments at the Centre and in those states had gone wrong and what could be done to retrieve the deteriorating situations, more specifically the prevailing level of alienation of the local population both in Jammu and Kashmir and the regions of the north-eastern states, e.g., Nagaland, Manipur, Mizoram, Tripura and Meghalaya in particular. The role and functions of the Intelligence Bureau and some other Central agencies also cropped up during discussion which lasted for about two hours. I also mentioned to Mr Gupta the names of at least half a dozen serving and retired IAS and IPS officers in and around Delhi, who could be trusted to give him the latest updates on the above issues, if necessary.

As I was taking leave of him, Indrajit Gupta thanked me for my views and 'useful' suggestions and said: "Mr Mukherjee, I am an old man and may not be able to digest and keep in mind all the points mentioned by you. Hence, may I request you to take further trouble by jotting down those points which may act as an aide memoir to me?" I agreed to do so and give it to him the next morning around 11 am since he had to return to Delhi within the next couple of days. He came out to see me off at the gate and asked me to request, on his behalf, my wife also to come to their house tomorrow so that he could introduce his wife to us and also have lunch together in his house.

When my wife and I arrived at his house the next morning, both he and Mrs Gupta received us and took us in. We spent about an hour during the course of which Mr and Mrs Gupta regaled us with many interesting and amusing facets of their lives, besides enquiring about my wife's past and current academic activities, about our children and so on. Thereafter I spent sometime separately with Mr. Gupta, handed over to him the 3-4 page note which I had prepared for him the previous night on our computer; followed by some further discussion on the points mentioned in my note. We learnt during lunch that all the food items on the table, nothing extravagant but simple Indian cuisine, were prepared by Mrs Gupta herself.

We may recall here that the 11th Lok Sabha elections, along with Assembly elections in six states, were held on April 27, May 7 and May 21, 1996. The Bharatiya Janata Party (BJP) surprised most political analysts by emerging as the single largest party with 161 seats. The Congress led by Narasimha Rao did not fare well. With no party securing a clear majority, the 11th Lok Sabha was destined to be a hung Parliament. Meanwhile, there were hectic activities among the remaining assortment of political parties. A disparate group of 13 such non-Congress and non-BJP parties formed a 'third alternative' forum known as the United Front[2] which could cobble up a total of 187 seats.

The UF constituents wanted Jyoti Basu to head the coalition government by virtue of his long experience in running a coalition government in West Bengal, besides his other known credentials, far exceeding those of any other political leader in the newly formed United Front. Accordingly, the UF leaders approached the prominent leaders of the CPM and others in the West Bengal Left Front, most of whom including Jyoti Basu happened to be in Delhi. Surprisingly, the majority of the CPM Politbureau members did not agree to such a proposal though CPM General Secretary Harkishen Singh Surjit and even Jyoti Basu were in favour of the UF proposal. In later years and perhaps in hindsight, Jyoti Basu correctly diagnosed this negative approach of his party's Politbureau/Central Committee as a 'Himalayan blunder'!

Eventually, on 14th May, 1996, HD Deve Gowda was selected as the compromise candidate and the same day he was elected as the leader of UF's Parliamentary Party. The leaders of the United Front called on the President the same evening to hand over their written support in favour of Deve Gowda and requested the President to call upon Deve Gowda to form the UF Government.

Some more drama was yet to unfold as the President Dr Shankar Dayal Sharma called upon the leader of the single largest party in Parliament, namely, Atal Behari Vajpayee of BJP to form the Government and also to prove its majority on the floor of Parliament. On May 16, 1996 Vajpayee was sworn in as Prime Minister, Lal Krishna Advani as Deputy PM and some other BJP MPs as Ministers. While the Confidence Vote moved by the new PM was being debated in the Lok Sabha on 27–28 May, Vajpayee realised that he was not going to win the confidence vote and hence he abruptly ended his speech in Parliament on 28th by announcing that he would be meeting the President, the same evening to tender his resignation.

On receipt of Vajpayee's resignation letter, the President called upon Deve Gowda, leader of the next largest parliamentary group, to form the Government. Accordingly on 1st June, 1996, Deve Gowda was sworn in as Prime Minister along with twenty other Ministers of his Government. The new PM moved a motion in Parliament on June 10 for a vote of confidence which was adopted by voice vote on June 12, the Congress party having decided to abstain from attending the Lok Sabha on those two days.

Then followed further discussions among the constituents of the United Front during the next few days as Indrajit Gupta wanted to be sworn in only along with the remaining MPs to be inducted as new ministers. This took place on June 28 when Indrajit Gupta was sworn in along with Chaturanan Mishra, Srikanta Jena, RL Jalappa and ten others.

However, Indrajit Gupta declined to take over charge as the Union Home Minister unless a certain Minister of State in the Home Ministry, already inducted by the PM, was removed from the Home Ministry since there were serious criminal charges pending against him in courts. The person concerned had to resign and then only Indrajit Gupta took charge as the new Home Minister. We wonder if any other Home Minister or even Prime Minister could demonstrate such courage of conviction.

A life-long Communist becoming the Home Minister, virtually the Number Two in the cabinet hierarchy, was indeed unprecedented, but this added to the stature and credibility of India's parliamentary democracy and it was hailed by all segments of the Indian Parliament solely due to the unquestioned respect which Indrajit Gupta had enjoyed over the past few decades of his long and unblemished parliamentary career.

On June 30, I rang up Indrajit Gupta to congratulate him as our new Home Minister but learnt that he was attending some urgent meeting in his Parliament House Chamber. Later the same day, he himself rang me back and wanted to know when I would be coming over to Delhi. This was a surprise for me and I told him so since there was no discussion with me regarding my moving over to Delhi. He again rang me up on 9th July 1996, asking me to come over to Delhi as early as possible and assume charge as Adviser to the Home Minister. I was not quite prepared mentally to shift to Delhi once again after having settled down in the peaceful surroundings of Salt Lake City. However, the issue was clinched when early next morning Indrajit Gupta again came on the line, this time from his Western Court residence, wanting to know the flight number by which I would be reaching

Delhi so that one of his officers could receive me at Delhi Airport. Thus I landed up in Delhi on July 14, 1996 and moved into room no. 104 in the West Bengal State Guest House, namely, Banga Bhavan, 3, Hailey Road[3].

Bathanitola Massacre of Dalits

As could be expected, I became part of the HM's hectic schedule from the very next day since the Parliament was in session - HM's briefing meetings with MHA officers regarding Parliament Questions and so on. Meanwhile, information was received regarding a dastardly massacre of some Dalit families in an isolated cluster of mud huts in a place called Bathanitola in the district of Jehanabad, Bihar. As could be expected, the new Home Minister Indrajit Gupta was truly outraged at the reported inaction of Bihar administration even after a lapse of 2-3 days.

Neither the Bihar Chief Minister Lalu Prasad Yadav nor any of his ministers, not to speak of the State's Chief Secretary, Home Secretary or the Director General of Police had cared to visit the carnage site till then. Quite expectedly, and true to his form, the Home Minister expressed his anguish when he spoke to the Bihar Chief Minister on July 16 and informed the latter about his proposed visit to Bathanitola on the following day, i.e. July 17. He made it clear to the Chief Minister that since the latter had not visited the carnage site so far, he may as well not accompany the Home Minister to Bathanitola[4] but should visit the affected village on any earliest date after the Home Minister's visit. The message was loud and clear and typical of Indrajit Gupta's forthright manner of speaking.

While inspecting the burnt down and ravaged huts of all the Dalit families at Bathanitola along with the

HM, I could spot a few policemen on the verandah of a brick-built house, obviously belonging to some upper caste landowner; the house was located on a high ground within a distance of about 50 yards of the carnage site and having a clear, unobstructed view of the ravaged site. As a former policeman myself, I was curious to know what role these policemen posted in this police outpost played during the carnage lasting for an hour or more, and hence I went over to the police post. On being asked why they did not intervene to stop the carnage which took place clearly within their sight, their response, though unambiguous, was truly beyond my imagination: "*Saab, hamara kam to lash uthana tha..*". (Sir, our task was to collect the dead bodies...').

When I narrated the above to the Home Minister after rejoining him near the burnt down and ravaged village, he too was equally stunned and enquired as to what I proposed to do. All I could say was that when we meet the Chief Minister and his senior officers on our return to Patna, I would narrate to them this shocking abdication of administrative responsibility, hoping that it would induce in them some sense of urgency, leading to the required administrative and legal remedial measures.

In our meeting at Patna Airport on return from Bathanitola, in which half a dozen top level IAS and IPS officers were present besides the Chief Minister, I did bring out in vivid details all that we had seen and heard including the shocking utterances of the police constables at the nearby outpost. I was perhaps too naïve to think that this would inject the desired sense of urgency in the Bihar government in preventing such episodes. I also remember to have strongly urged the CM as the '*Masiha* of the dalits' (Saviour of the dalits) to urgently introduce drastic land reforms measures on the West Bengal model as one of the long-term solutions. Obviously, Indrajit Gupta knew better. When we were returning to Delhi the same evening by a BSF plane, the Home Minister expressed the view that he was yet to come across a Bihar politician who would dare to antagonise the powerful *Bhumihars* (landholders) by implementing any drastic land reform measures on the West Bengal pattern. Perhaps this holds good even today!

Dealing with a 'recalcitrant' Home Minister

> *Why should these VIP security experts think that anybody would be in the least interested in doing away with Indrajit Gupta, even if he happens to be the Home Minister?... Don't you think our country would perhaps be better off without nearly half of the VVIPs/ VIPs spread all over the country, costing several hundred, if not thousands of crores of rupees of public money !...*

Generally speaking, every Home Minister has a certain degree of security risk and as such the Intelligence Bureau of the Government of India and the Delhi Police have some specified drill for the Home Minister's security at his residence, office as also during his movements within and outside Delhi. That is why his official residence is carefully selected by a joint team of Intelligence Bureau and Delhi Police officers in keeping with the security requirements. But neither the Director, IB nor Delhi's Commissioner of Police could persuade the new Home Minister to move into the sprawling bungalow in Lutyen's Delhi which was readied for him, with requisite specifications of depth.

As an old Member of Parliament, he was staying in one of the two-room flats in Western Court (off Janpath), one of the old residential complexes for the MPs. Purely on genuine security reasons, the DIB and the CP, Delhi tried their best to persuade the Home Minister to shift to the earmarked and security-vetted bungalow but to no avail. Some days after I joined as the HM's Adviser, these officers, who had known me for long, met me and sought my help in persuading the Home Minister. Having myself dealt with such VIP security matters in the past, I agreed with their proposition and promised to do my best.

The same evening I had prolonged discussion with Indrajit Gupta on this issue in his Western Court flat and mentioned that he did not have to move into the HM's official residence to add to his glory or glamour but for other more mundane reasons, the judgement for which should better be left to the professional experts in such matters. Typical of him, Indrajit Gupta came out with his counter-arguments, somewhat on these lines: "Why should these VIP security experts think that anybody would be in the least interested in doing away with Indrajit Gupta, even if he happens to be the Home Minister? I am indeed grateful to you and the others for your genuine concern just as I agree with your and the security experts' viewpoints. But don't you think that our country would perhaps be better off without nearly half the VVIPs/VIPS spread all over the country costing several hundred, if not thousands of crores of rupees of public money–the money which could be spent for feeding lakhs of our countrymen who do not get even a single square meal a day ?...".

There was no way in which one could rebut even a fraction of what he said in this vein and I could feel that he was saying all this not to impress me, for, that was not his nature either. He was speaking straight from the heart. As a last ditch effort, I urged him fairly strongly that he should not persist in giving sleepless nights to those officers who are charged with the extremely sensitive and onerous responsibility of providing the best of humanly possible security to at least certain categories of VVIPs and VIPS, irrespective of the person holding such posts. He countered by stating that neither Indira Gandhi as the then Prime Minister nor her son Rajiv Gandhi , who was the Prime Minister till the other day, could be saved in spite of the maximum possible security having been provided to them.

I countered by saying that Indira Gandhi's assassination was possible, as subsequent inquiries revealed, largely because the security arrangements were thoughtlessly altered and tampered with by some person/persons, ignoring the views of the experts charged with the task of her security. Likewise Rajiv Gandhi's assassination could be attributed to the callous disregard to his threat perception by withdrawing his SPG cover on the criminally negligent plea that, under the provision of the SPG Act then, only the Prime Minister, and not a former PM, was entitled to SPG protection! Wasn't the SPG Act amended almost overnight, after such a national tragedy, to provide SPG cover not only to successive functioning Prime Ministers and former PMs but also to hordes of their family members, many with dubious reputations?

Even if the legal technicality was considered to be so sacrosanct, couldn't the purpose be served by detailing for Rajiv Gandhi's protection the same set of SPG officers under some other nomenclature because these officers knew over-time the plus and minus points of the protectee's personality traits which become crucial in providing the irreducible level of security cover?

Another set of equally trained officers could be termed as the Special Protection Group (SPG) almost overnight and detailed for the functioning PM without making any fuss about it. There was no dearth of such specially trained officers within the SPG family itself then or later.

When all my efforts to overcome Indrajit Gupta's resistance to moving into his officially earmarked residence with built-in security arrangements failed even after nearly a couple of hour's discussion with him, we had to devise some alternative scheme. For this, I had a detailed discussion with the DIB and Delhi's Police Commissioner along with their principal security experts the same night to explore the best possible alternative arrangement. It was finally agreed by these security experts that next morning they will have a discreet recce of the Western Court to devise alternative security arrangements for the HM's residence. As desired by the DIB and the CP/Delhi, I joined them at Western Court for a final round of discussion with them. It was agreed that one of the MPs occupying an adjacent flat would be persuaded to shift to a more commodious accommodation and part of the vacant flat could be utilised as the HM's camp office, besides providing the scope for access control to this area. Eventually, the arrangement proved to be the best possible alternative security arrangement for, perhaps, the first ever 'recalcitrant' Home Minister of India !

HM's visit to Jammu and Kashmir

Indrajit Gupta was understandably worried at petty ego clashes among the security forces. He strongly felt that during a period of substantially reduced level of violence (in J&K), the leaders of security forces should devote their entire energy towards winning the hearts and minds of the local people…

Meanwhile, there was some lessening in the militant violence in Jammu and Kashmir but we kept receiving some disturbing information about the continuing bickerings among those charged with the responsibility of internal security in the state - the army *vis-à-vis* the Governor, former Army Chief General KV Krishna Rao as also between the local army brass and the state agencies, the BSF and the CRPF. The army had been insisting for long that all other security agencies should function under their command and control.

This was obviously not acceptable to others and the Home Ministry too was not agreeable. It was further learnt that there was a lot of resentment even among the senior army commanders in J&K against the Governor who, it was alleged, used to treat such senior commanders in a cavalier fashion as if he was still the Army Chief and these senior commanders were nothing more than colonels and brigadiers, and not Lt Generals or Major Generals.

Home Minister Indrajit Gupta was understandably worried at such petty ego clashes among the security forces. He strongly felt that during such period of substantially reduced level of violence, the leaders of all such forces should devote their entire energy towards winning the hearts and minds of the local people in real terms and not just as a superficial rhetoric or public relations exercise. This emerged during a couple of rounds of my informal discussions with the Home Minister in Delhi itself, and this prompted him to decide about an early visit to the state to study the situation there by meeting not only the functionaries of state, army, BSF, CRPF, etc., but also many of the members of the public and political leaders. Accordingly a two-day schedule was drawn up for 8th/9th August, 1996.

The first engagement of the HM on August 8, 1996 was at the Army Command HQ at Srinagar which was attended by Lt. Gen. Saklani and other senior army officers, the J&K Chief Secretary and DGP, the DGs of BSF and CRPF and a few others representing the intelligence agencies. They were asked to give their assessment about the state's internal security scenario region-wise, the problems faced by them and their suggestions as to how best the prevailing atmosphere of peace and tranquility could be strengthened.

Such encouragement by the Home Minister to all the officers to speak out frankly and in an unbiased manner produced the desired results, revealing their strengths and weaknesses as also the best possible means to achieve the twin objectives, namely, to develop greater rapport with the local population and simultaneously to ensure the fullest possible security of the different regions of the state. Besides other things, this meeting led some of us to think in terms of devising an inclusive mechanism for the harmonious functioning of all relevant agencies[5] charged with the responsibility of ensuring internal security.

Unexpected Revelation in Baramula

For nearly 6-7 years, the Sikhs started moving out of their homes in Baramula with their families, apprehending threat from across the PoK which was close by, despite exhortations by their neighbours not to do so. Most such Sikhs with their family members were living in refugee camps in Jammu and other nearby places. Exemplary display of true Kashmiriyaat by the Muslim neighbours of the Sikhs provided surprise galore when they started returning to Baramula!

Baramula district, close to the PoK (Pakistan-occupied Kashmir) and the LoC, was traditionally known to be the hot-spot of violence and militancy. Typical of Indrajit Gupta, he desired to meet the local people in Baramula itself, irrespective of their political or other affiliations. Perhaps no Home Minister ever thought of doing so till then. This meeting was arranged in the spacious Town Hall, with its beautifully crafted and ornate wooden ceiling. By the time we arrived there from Srinagar on 8th August 1996 afternoon, the hall was overflowing with people, some even standing on the lawns outside. After his brief introductory observations, congratulating the local people for their role in maintaining peace in the area, the HM invited them to speak about their problems of daily life and also to suggest measures for development of the area.

The meeting was halfway through when I noticed, being seated on the left of the HM on a slightly raised platform, at least 6-8 Sikhs with their traditional beards and turbans among the people present in the hall. I was not quite sure if these gentlemen were local residents or were brought in to fill the hall! I quietly slipped out of the hall, went outside, spotted a local organiser and requested him to discreetly call out one or two of the Sikh gentlemen from the hall.

What transpired thereafter was truly revealing. We all knew that Baramula was not only the starting point but also the focal point of separatist violence in the Valley during the late 1980s and early 1990s which led to large-scale exodus of not only the Kashmiri Pandits but also other non-Muslims like the Sikhs. After talking to these two Sardarjis and thereafter to some others also, I learnt that most of them were shopkeepers or other small businessmen or farmers, that they were residents of Baramula with their family members for long - till violence gripped the area, mostly indulged in by some people who generally belonged to PoK on the other side of the LoC. Their neighbours, all Muslims, were unhappy when they decided to leave but assured them of doing, whatever little they could to protect their homes, shops, etc. For nearly 6-7 years they took shelter in the 'refugee camps' in and around Jammu but tried to maintain periodic contact with their neighbours through some emissaries. During the past 2-3 years, they were receiving messages from their neighbours, urging them to come back. Two of them decided to return, without their family members, just to study the ground reality. To their utter surprise, they found that not only their houses but their shops too were undamaged. When they opened their shops, another round of surprise was in store for them - not a single item of the goods in their shops was missing or damaged!

At this point of their narration, I enquired, out of natural curiosity, "What was your response?" What was revealed thereafter was equally touching: all of them wanted to freely distribute all their goods in their shops among their neighbours but the latter would not agree to it, saying that, whatever they did was only to be expected from any good neighbour. This, I felt, was the true spirit of Kashmiriyaat which our self-seeking leaders have utterly failed to appreciate and capitalise on for building a truly resurgent J&K which could make us proud all over our country.

Very recently I came across a fascinating book on Kashmir, an autobiographical account by a young Kashmiri journalist named Basharat Peer *Curfewed Night*, 2008, Random House India[6]. It has already received some very commendatory and well-deserved reviews by persons like Khuswant Singh ("...It is beautifully written, brutally honest and deeply hurtful. It needed courage to write it"), Tavleen Singh ("An important book–for a change we hear the story of what happened in the past fifteen years, told in a genuine Kashmiri voice") and also by Ahmed Rashid ("The story of Kashmir has never been told before so evocatively and profoundly. Peer writes with the skill of a novelist, the insight of a journalist and the evocative powers of a poet)".

When I told the HM about the above episode concerning some Sikh residents of Baramula and quite possibly elsewhere too in J&K, unknown to us, he too was genuinely impressed and repeated this episode at many places to bring home the best lesson of our visit to J&K. I keep wondering even now if we will ever learn the correct lesson which alone could be the greatest antidote to our divisive politics not only in J&K but elsewhere in the country as well.

On August 9, 1996 we went down to Jammu where the HM visited most of the camps where the migrants from the Valley, mostly Kashmiri Pandits, had been residing. They were understandably resentful about the apathy of the administration. HM's visit to far off Doda in the mountainous region and his interactions with the local people brought out similar popular anguish against the administration's lack of concern for these people.

HM's visits to Bulgaria and Russia

The Bulgarian gentleman accompanying us during our tour of Bulgaria informed us that after the end of the Communist regime and the resultant 'de-collectivisation of lands', nobody knew to whom these lands originally belonged because old land records were no longer in existence. Hence, none came forward for cultivation of these lands !

Sometime during early October,1996, invitations were received by the HM from his counterparts in Russia and Bulgaria for official visits to these countries. These were followed by visits of the embassy officials of these two countries to the Home Ministry in North Block to work out the details of the visit schedules. Besides Indrajit Gupta as the Indian Home Minister, his party consisted of his wife Mrs Gupta, the Special Secretary of the Home Ministry, VS Mathur, HM's Private Secretary, Dr SB Singh, and myself, Adviser to HM.

We left Delhi Airport by the Lufthansa flight in the early hours of October 30, 1996, reaching Frankfurt around 11.50 hours IST. Since the connecting flight of Balkan Airlines was nearly 7 hours later, the Indian Consul General at Frankfurt, Partha Sarathi Roy, enquired if the HM would like to visit the historic city and its famed University at Heidelberg. Having been an avid student of History, he readily agreed to do so and as such we all left by road, looked up quite a few of the places of historical interest including the old Bridge and the Castle, the Old and New University of Heidelberg.

This, however, was my second visit to Heidelberg, the first one being in 1988 when I was the Additional Director of CBI in New Delhi. This was on an invitation from the History Department of the Heidelberg University for taking a seminar on the subject of 'Scarcity & Crime', one of the topics of my Ph D dissertation. During the 1988 visit I learnt that Heidelberg was the only city in Germany which was not bombed by the Allied forces. Why was Heidelberg spared, I enquired, while the rest of

Germany was virtually bombed out? According to some historians, the old teacher of the chief of the British Royal Air Force was a professor of Heidelberg University who lived in this city and the RAF chief had obtained special approval of Prime Minister Winston Churchill to ensure that his old teacher was not harmed in any way. Thus, the entire city and its environs remained undamaged by the ravages of World War-II!

We arrived at Bulgaria's capital city of Sofia from Frankfurt the same evening. On October 31, we attended the Home Minister's scheduled meetings with the Bulgarian Interior Minister Dobrev and the Minister of Justice Chervenyakov and their senior officers. In between, our Home Minister attended a function at the Indira Gandhi School near Sofia where he was requested to unveil a statue of Bhagat Singh–a martyr in the cause of India's freedom movement. An official dinner was hosted the same night by the Bulgarian Interior Minister at Boyana for the Indian Home Minister, his wife Mrs Gupta and all members of the delegation.

The next day our HM had a hectic schedule of meetings with their Foreign Affairs Minister Pirinsky, Trade and Foreign Economic Co-operation Minister Paparizov, Bulgarian Prime Minister Z Videnov and the Minister of Industry, L Datchev. The same night, there was a Dinner hosted by the Indian Ambassador Nirupama Sen for some Bulgarian dignitaries along with the Indian Home Minister and his delegation members.

November 2nd started with a visit to the well-known arms factory 'Arsenal' at Kazanlak. This visit was perhaps scheduled to arouse India's interest in placing some bulk orders for purchases but our HM showed no interest whatsoever. Moreover, we found the sprawling factory site in a dismal state of maintenance and repairs and it appeared as though not much of productive activity had been taking place in the recent past.

At this point, I may narrate an interesting episode en route. We had left Sofia around 9.30 in the morning on way to Kazanlak, nearly two and half hour's journey, in a convoy of about four cars–an escort car with some of their security personnel, followed by a car in which Mr and Mrs Gupta were travelling along with a liaison officer; the third car had VS Mathur, Special Secretary of our Home Ministry and myself along with our liaison officer and the next car had the HM's Private Secretary, Dr SB Singh and an officer of the Indian Embassy.

On the way, I was quite surprised to see that miles after miles of agricultural land on both sides of the road were lying fallow. I was curious to find out why it was so, especially when the Bulgarian economy was known to be in a bad shape. Hence, I stopped our car midway, which prompted the two other cars ahead of us by a couple of hundred yards drive backwards towards our car, thinking that something might have gone wrong with our car. The HM as well as his liaison officer and those in the escort car also came out and started enquiring if anything had gone wrong with our car.

I told them that nothing was wrong with the car or ourselves but discreetly referred to my 'curiosity' about the reasons for which such vast tracts of apparently fertile agricultural land were not being put under cultivation. It could be gathered from these Bulgarian gentlemen that after the end of the Communist regime and resultant 'de-collectivisation of lands', nobody knew to whom the lands initially belonged because old land records were no longer in existence ! Hence none came forward for cultivation of these tracts of land. It appeared from my talks with these gentlemen that the state too was not taking any initiative for 'lack of resources'–a queer situation indeed: a stagnant economy both in terms of industrial and agricultural production, shortage of food for the people and yet such unbelievably large tracts of land lying fallow! Sometime later the same day, I mentioned this phenomenon to our visiting Home Minister Indrajit Gupta and came up with an apparently outlandish suggestion of mine: whether the Government of India could offer to 'export' a large body of agricultural experts and farmers from India for a 3-5 year contract, equipped with necessary inputs like tractors, fertilisers, etc., which could be beneficial to both Bulgaria and India.

His response was somewhat like this: 'I appreciate your concern and your simple but workable solution. I will try to sell your suggestion at our appropriate quarters but my gut feeling is that there would hardly be any takers in either country even for such a workable and beneficial proposition'. And the wisdom of Indrajit Gupta proved right[7].

On to Russia

On the morning of November 4, 1996 we left Sofia for Moscow where an impressive reception was held at the Presidential Lounge of the Sheremetevo-2 Airport, which was attended by the Deputy Minister of Interior Lt General PM Latyshev, Mme Kulikova, wife of the Russian Interior Minister Gen AS Kulikov and several others, besides the Indian Ambassador, Ronen Sen, and his wife. Regarding the absence of the Interior Minister Gen AS Kulikov from the reception, it transpired, informally though, that due to the serious illness of the

Russian President Boris Yeltsin, hospitalised perhaps the same morning or previous evening, an intense power struggle had started about the possible successor and that Kulikov was supposed to be a powerful contender too.

The HM and his wife along with the rest of his delegation were put up at the plush and sprawling Dacha No 8 at the famed Serebryany Bor, the entire area known to be under the control of the Interior Ministry.

The same afternoon, the HM had scheduled meetings with AI Nikolayev, Head of the Federal Border Guards Service of Russia and VI Trubnikov, Director of the Foreign Intelligence Service of Russia, the two other powerful personalities besides Kulikov, at the famous Lubyanka and Kolpachni Pereulok respectively. I had the privilege of accompanying the HM to all these meetings in which the Indian Ambassador or someone from our Embassy acted as an interpreter.

On 4th November, a formal and lavish Dinner-cum-reception was hosted by the Interior Minister Kulikov, Napoleon-like in stature and looks. After a round of warm introductions and playing of the impressive musical band of the Interior Ministry, interspersed with drinks, the formal Dinner started with an unending 'introductory' rounds of toasts with vodka.

And such vodka toasts continued in between meals as well! I observed during the evening that, for some reasons unfathomable by me, the HM was somewhat off-colour and was rather circumspect even in drinking the customary toasts of vodka. We, however, were exercising the required circumspection in imbibing vodka, according to me, not a tasty drink at all, but without being noticed by others.

It was only later the next day that I had some inkling about the possible cause of Indrajit Gupta's rather gloomy or sulking demeanour at the Dinner. I had very innocuously, perhaps somewhat mischievously, mentioned that the opulence and luxury provided even in the Dacha where we were housed far surpassed these available in any five star hotel in any part of the Western World and as such the luxurious life style of the Russian leaders was unimaginable by the common Russian citizens - earlier or even then.

And I also puckishly but somewhat innocently enquired if during the dozens of visits to Russia in the 1970s and 1980s by him and/or the other important leaders of the Communist Party of India, they were ever accommodated in any such Dacha. As could be expected from Indrajit Gupta, who was never known for any superficial sugar-coating in giving vent to his emotions, either of anger or of affection, burst out with some choicest expletives against the Russian leadership of the past decades and stated that he could never forgive them for having 'betrayed' the cause of the 'great' Russian revolution.

Next morning, we learnt that President Boris Yeltsin had undergone a triple by-pass heart surgery around 7 am. Hence, HM's scheduled meeting with the head of the Russian Federal Security Services, ND Kovalyov, could take place somewhat late in the famed Lybyanskaya Ploschad, followed by a more than an hour-long meeting with the Russian Interior Minister, General AS Kulikov and his key officers in his office. Thereafter, we retired to our place of stay in the Dacha for a private lunch. The same afternoon, we took a walk in the famous Kremlin Mall, before going over to the Dinner hosted by the Indian

Ambassador Ronen Sen. The other guests included the General Secretary of the Russian Communist Party and a few others, mostly members of the Indian business community in Russia.

During my informal interactions with the Indians, especially with the Indian business community, I came to know of a few interesting features of life in Russia then and Moscow in particular:

(a) The Russian mafia gangs, not all underground, were quite pervasive and had gathered strength during the Yeltsin years of rule but nobody would dare to admit this nor was there any sign of the government cracking down on them[8].

(b) Surprisingly, there was a fairly strong Indian mafia too, specially in and around Moscow, This came as a big surprise to us. However, it transpired, on my further queries, that their initial targets were the Indians living in Russia; businessmen, representatives of Indian industrial houses and Indian public sector undertakings, even the very large number of Indian students were not spared the extortion rackets run by the Indian gangs. Another surprising revelation was that most of the members of the Indian mafia gangs were of Bihar origin-'exported from Bihar', as some of them mentioned gleefully!

In the forenoon of 6th November, Indrajit Gupta's scheduled meeting with Dr IP Rybkin, Secretary of the Russian Security Council and his officers took place at Staraya Ploschard, followed by a visit to the Lenin Mausoleum in Kremlin and a walk around the famed Red Square and some nearby places. When we retired to our Dacha for lunch, we were informed that the meeting with the Russian Prime Minister in the afternoon was cancelled due to the PM's preoccupation with the transfer of power to him by the ailing President Yeltsin. A story was circulating in Moscow that the all-important 'Black Box', containing the key to Russia's nuclear arsenal, had to be forcibly snatched from the ailing Yeltsin for its transfer to his successor!

A joint Press Conference was held by our HM along with his Russian counterpart Gen Kulikov as scheduled. The same evening we were taken to the famed Bolshoi Theatre where we witnessed the ballet performance "Taming of the Shrew" along with Gen. Kulikov, his wife Madam Kulikova and the Indian Ambassador Ronen Sen and his wife.

The next day on November 7, was a real treat for us, the first-time visitors to Russia. The Russian Interior Minister's big and lavishly furnished jet plane took us to St Petersberg, capital of the Czarist Russia, later renamed as Leningrad during the Soviet Communist Regime and still later called Stalingrad, depending on who the reigning deity of the Soviet regime was during the relevant period. After the break-up of the Soviet Russia, it was rechristened as St Petersberg.

From the Pulkovo Airport of St Petersberg, we were taken straight to the Victory Square for laying wreaths at the massive 'Monument to City Defenders'. During World War II, the Nazi Army, despite heavy loss of lives on their side too, the Germans laid a siege to the city for 900 days - nearly for three years! And in a rare feat of heroism against extreme adversity, the Russian men, women and children besides the ragtag Red Army continued to put up stiff resistance, day and night, to prevent the invading Nazi German Army from entering the heart of the city. A well-preserved and fully documented history of this rare saga of heroism and sacrifice of the Russian people could be seen in the sprawling war museum in its basement Hall of the Monument.

After a short visit to the famed Peter and Paul Fortress, we retired for a couple of hours to Hotel Astoria and it was a great relief, howsoever short, from the biting cold and the arctic wind (gale, really!) about which our HM had warned me in Delhi itself when I expressed a desire to visit the historic city of St Petersberg. We had a post-lunch meeting with the Governor of St Petersberg, Mr Yakovlev, at the historic Smolney Palace, from where Lenin launched and organised the first phase of the Russian Revolution. At one end of the Palace, we could visit Lenin's study-cum-rest room, a rather small cubicle with a small wooden writing desk, a chair and a small bed, indicative of the Spartan life style of one of the main initiators of the Russian Revolution–which stood in sharp contrast to the opulent life style of its leaders.

It was an unpleasant surprise when I learnt that a visit to the world famous Hermitage Museum of St Petersberg was not on our itinerary and that we were slated for dinner in about an hour's time in an Indian restaurant "Tandoor"; thereafter we were to go to the airport for our return journey to Moscow. When I mentioned this 'glaring omission' to Mr Gupta, he glared at me and said 'You would only see the signs of opulence of the Czarist Russia- golden and gold- rested thrones, gold-plated chairs and palanquins, thousands of costly tapestries and carpets in addition to several thousand paintings in gold-bordered frames and realise why the Communist revolutionaries dethroned him...'. I did not have the heart to ask him whether the Czar and the whole family deserved to be brutally murdered by the 'revolutionaries', not sparing even the women and their children !

However, in deference to my wishes, it was quickly arranged with the help of one of our Russian liaison officers so that Mathur and I could pay at least a short visit to the famed Hermitage Museum. Thanks to the Director of the Museum, the old gentleman was kind enough to take us round some of the halls and also explained in some details about the exhibits so that laymen like us could learn at least the basic facts about those exhibits. We could be there hardly for two hours or so, whereas one would need, we were told, anything from seven to ten days just to have a look at all the exhibits and need many more days to have a proper understanding and feel of the sprawling complex, euphemistically called the 'Hermitage' Museum and its magnificent exhibits!

On the morning of 8th November, we were to visit the Troitse-Sergiev Monastery of the Russian Orthodox Church, a few kilometres outside Moscow. It was only in the morning that Mr Gupta informed us that he and his wife would not be able to visit the monastery. This caused acute embarrassment to us since we had information that the Russian Interior Minister General Kulikov, his wife and daughter would be waiting for us at a certain road crossing so that we all could visit the monastery together.

Mathur and I had to come up with some 'plausible' excuse for the absence of Mr Gupta and his wife. The local Mayor and the chief of the local Militia received us, apart from the head of the monastery. We could see how very eagerly the Kulikov family was looking forward to this visit, especially Madam Kulikova and their young daughter. The priests and other functionaries of the monastery were obviously happy that such a high Russian dignitary and his family members were enjoying this visit. They had arranged an elaborate lunch for us at the monastery.

However, I returned to our Dacha with a bitter taste in the mouth at Mr Gupta's failure to honour the sentiments of his local host. Was it due to his aversion to such signs of incipient 'religious revivalism' in Russia? Or could it be that they were truly indisposed on our return from St Petersberg late last night? If it was the former, I would have considered it bad enough, for we could not even pretend to be their moral guardians; if it was the second factor responsible for their inability, I failed to get a clear idea even after making my unhappy feelings known to Mr Gupta. Either way, I looked back at this episode with a feeling of sadness - more so as he was admittedly a very cultured and civilised personality otherwise.

It was known that Mr Gupta remained a bachelor well past his middle age and married a Muslim lady named Begum Suraiya after she was separated from her husband. She had two (?) daughters from her earlier marriage - one of them used to live with her husband Mr Naidu in the first floor of Shri Gupta's ancestral house at Dover Road in Calcutta and the other daughter lived in Bombay with her husband and two children. Whenever, the Bombay-based daughter with her children came to stay for a few days in Mr Gupta's Western Court flat, one could see how very happy Mr Gupta was, especially in the company of the grand children, as if they were his own children and grand children. This tender facet of Mr Gupta's personality, with an otherwise rough exterior, was a fascinating experience for me to witness on a couple of occasions.

Revival of Police Reforms, initiatives by Indrajit Gupta

The MHA affidavit filed in the Supreme Court in response to a PIL seeking implementation of the National Police Commission recommendations was not even shown to Indrajit Gupta. After coming to know about this from me, he ordered immediate withdrawal of the same and submission of a fresh one after getting approved by him.

At this stage I would like to refer to the role played by Home Minister Indrajit Gupta with regard to the long neglected issue of police reform, especially for two reasons: Firstly, it is generally accepted as somewhat characteristic of an Indian Communist to be inherently 'allergic' to police; it is believed to be the legacy of their anti-establishment movements of the fifties and sixties of the 20th century when clashes with police were frequent.

Indrajit Gupta could not be expected by me to be an exception, till I had occasion to interact with him closely about the history and the imperatives of police reform–the overriding objective being to transform the Indian police from its continuing role as a tool in the hands of their controllers, political and bureaucratic, into one of being the agent of the community and the common citizens. After days of discussions with me on the subject, it did not take him long to come to the basics of a meaningful police reform with greater social accountability on the part of police. Secondly, once he felt convinced about the urgency and parameters of the reform agenda, he went all out to lend his strong support for the same, as would be revealed in course of the subsequent narrative.

Police all over the world is considered to be a status-quoist organisation both in respect of the system which policemen are required to protect. More specifically, any attempt at police reform should not only aim at changing the police system but also the laws governing them. Some of us in police, in the so-called 'elitist and privileged' Indian Police Service, holding fairly high and comfortable positions in our respective organisations of police, decided to break new grounds for police as a whole. Thus, in one of the periodical meetings of the Central IPS Association, which represented all state and Central Police Organisations, we decided to urge the Central Government to set up a high-powered Commission to dissect the maladies besetting police which should then come up with suitable remedial measures to make the police truly community-oriented instead of continuing to be ruler-oriented as a result of the prevailing laws and rules governing police all over India. With the above end in view, we as representatives of the Central IPS Association called on Prime Minister/successive Home Ministers between 1974 and 1976 and were told that the matter would be 'looked into in due course'. We knew that nothing of the sort was taking place, largely because no government, either at the centre or in the states, wanted to loosen their grip over police which they continued to utilise and misuse through pliable and quite often unscrupulous policemen to protect their partisan purposes as against the needs of the common citizens.

In the wake of the post-Emergency governmental upheaval, a new government came into being in 1977 at the Centre with Morarji Desai as Prime Minister and Charan Singh as Deputy Prime Minister and Home Minister. Desai was known to be a strong status-quoist and as such we in the Central IPS Association felt that it would be futile to expect him to tread the path of basic police reform. On the contrary, the Dy PM and HM Charan Singh, who had earlier been a Chief Minister of UP, though with a short stint, was known to be not only honest but was serious about ushering in good governance in the country, especially in the critical state of Uttar Pradesh - the biggest in geographical area and population as also contributing the largest number of MPs in Parliament. Moreover, in the face of serious political fall-out, he was learnt to have been fully supportive of his appointee chief of the State Police in UP, NS Saksena who, true to his known reputation for integrity and professionalism, went hammer and tong against many of the known police malpractices like corruption, minimisation/non-registration of cases including dacoities and robberies being shown as burglaries and thefts, murders as unnatural deaths, kowtowing to politicians for postings and transfers and so on. The inevitable outcome was that many of his MLAs, for long accustomed to misuse the police for personal aggrandizement, joined the other camps, resulting in the fall of the Charan Singh-led SVD (Samyukta Vidhayak Dal) Ministry.

We in the Central IPS Association decided to make a fresh bid for setting up of a National Police Commission for the purpose mentioned earlier and sought an appointment with the new Home Minister, with the one-point agenda as above. We decided on a five-member delegation: Hargovind Bhatnagar, DIG, BSF, AP Mukherjee - DIG, CBI, TA Chari, DIG, CRPF, Nikhil Kumar of Delhi Police and the previous Secretary of our Association and Gautam Kaul also of Delhi Police and the then Secretary of the Association. Traditionally, one of the very senior IPS officers heading the Central Police Organisations (IB, CBI, BSF, CRPF) used to be requested by the Association to be the leader of the delegation. Three of the top officers were approached by us in turn, explaining the basic purpose of this delegation of ours, and all three excused themselves on one pretext or the other. We realised that those 'wise' police leaders did not want to be associated with the 'young Turks', lest they incur the displeasure of the new government! It was then decided by us that the other senior police leader (NS Saksena, IP/1941/UP and then the DG of CRPF) would be requested to lead our delegation before the new Home Minister. Since I resided in the same area as Mr Saksena[9] and also knew him well as his morning walk companion, it fell to my lot to persuade him to be our delegation leader.

It did not take me long to explain our purpose and extend our request, which was readily accepted by him. Fortunately, it turned out to be the best possible choice since he was the Chief of UP Police when Charan Singh was the Chief Minister of UP and his reputation for personal and professional integrity was wellknown.

Thereafter, we five delegation members decided among ourselves in advance as to the aspects on which each one of us would speak, after our leader introduced the members and explained to the Home Minister that we were not seeking any benefits for the IPS or even for the police as a whole, that our only objective was for setting up of a high-powered National Commission to dissect the maladies besetting the police and consequently recommend appropriate remedial measures including replacing the archaic and ruler-oriented Indian Police Act of 1861 by a modern community-oriented Police Act. At the end of our presentations, the Home Minister asked us quite a few searching questions by way of further clarifications and finally said that he would try to do something about this issue, which he too agreed was a matter of national concern. However, knowing the negative attitude of quite a few bureaucrats in the Home Ministry and elsewhere, besides the utter reluctance of most politicians in power to loosen their grip over police for their petty and partisan interests, we were sceptical about the final outcome. Overcoming all possible objections and obstructive tactics, the upright and sturdy Jat that he was, Charan Singh succeeded in having the momentous first step by setting up the National Police Commission (NPC) with fairly wide and unambiguous terms of reference, with Dharma Vira, ex-ICS, a former Cabinet Secretary and Governors of 2-3 States, as Chairman and four other members.[10]

In the backdrop of the unprecedented revolt of the UP Provincial Armed Constabulary (PAC) in 1976-77, the First Report of the NPC, submitted in February, 1979 predictably was largely devoted to the issues of recruitment, training, working and living conditions of the Constabulary. The first part of the Second Report submitted in August, 1979 dealt with another important allied aspect, viz., welfare measures for the families of the subordinate ranks of police.

However, the Second Report went into some of the core issues of basic police reform, viz.,

- Police role, duties, powers and responsibilities in modern India.
- Interference with and misuse of police by illegal or improper orders or pressures from political executives or other extraneous sources.
- Remedial steps to reduce, if not eliminate, the baneful impact of the above on the lawfully enjoined investigative duties of police as also in disciplinary matters including even routine transfers and postings.
- Some steps to ensure professional and functional independence of police but within a system of

more effective and transparent accountability of the police at different levels. This was to be ensured through a multi-member State Security Commission.

- As a first step in that direction, the NPC recommended (a) transparent system of selection of the Police Chief of the State and (b) a fixed tenure of four years or for a period extending up to the date of his retirement in the normal course, and that (c) these were to be fixed statutorily.

The remaining six reports of the NPC dealt with other aspects of police functioning, viz. The police role and functions regarding the weaker sections of the society, village police, need for special law for dealing with serious and widespread breaches of public order, corruption in police, economic offences, need for modernisation of law enforcement [3rd Report, January 1980]:

- Investigation, court trial and prosecution agency, police role and functions in dealing with industrial and agrarian unrest [4th Report, June 1980];
- Recruitment of Constables and Sub-Inspectors of the civil police and their training along with specialised training of Inspectors of Police and Deputy Superintendents of Police, induction of greater number of Women Police, police-public relations as well as the relationship between the District Police and the Executive Magistracy, and the code of behaviour and conduct for police officers of all ranks [5th Report, November 1980].
- The police leadership and the changed role and career planning of the officers of the Indian Police Service, appropriate police role and functions in

dealing with communal riots and new orientation about urban policing tasks [6th Report, March 1981];

- Need for changes in the organisational structure of the police and greater delegation of financial powers to police officers at various levels on the pattern of such devolution in the central police organisations, changes required in the system of performance appraisal of police personnel [7th Report, May 1981].
- The 8th and Concluding Report [May 1981] further examined aspects of Accountability of Police Performance and also provided the detailed model of a new Police Act in place of the archaic Police Act of 1861, suited to the needs of a modern India; this Model Act was prepared painstakingly by a body of experts in law, administration and policing to usher in a fairly progressive, citizen-centric and fully accountable policing system.

What happened after all these painstaking work of the NPC is quite revealing. By the time all the reports of the NPC was submitted to the Government, Indira Gandhi had returned to power after decisively defeating all her political opponents. For some inexplicable reasons, a powerful section of the bureaucracy, both in the states and at the Centre, did not want any basic change in the policing system and in the Indian Police Act of 1861. Hence, primarily to thwart even the moderate changes recommended by the Commission headed by a renowned ICS officer Dharma Vira and knowing that the Emergency Excesses Commission (Shah Commission) was an anathema to Prime Minister Indira Gandhi, she was informed at the first available opportunity that the

NPC Reports contained quite a few references to the Shah Commission Report on Emergency excesses and sought her directive as to what steps could be taken on the NPC reports by the Government of India. The PM's response was on predictable lines as could be gauged by the wily bureaucrats: 'to throw the Reports into the waste paper basket' and not even to be shown to her! True to their usual modus operandi, the bureaucrats, especially in the Ministry of Home Affairs, 'forwarded' these NPC reports to the state governments 'for such action as was deemed appropriate since Police was a subject in the State List of the Constitution'!

However, as a measure of 'abundant caution' and to show that they were more loyal than the king (queen?), the officers mentioned in a separate paragraph of the above letter that those paragraphs of the NPC reports which contained references to the Shah Commission Report (on Emergency Excesses) were to be 'treated as cancelled and withdrawn by the Government of India'! This was indeed the classic example of bureaucratic guile and sycophancy even in a matter of serious national concern, viz., meaningful and some basic police reforms which the country and its citizens were legitimately hoping for after over three decades since Independence.

Indrajit Gupta's historic DO letter on Police Reforms

Nearly twenty years after the said treatment of the NPC reports, it fell to my lot in 1997 as the Advisor to the Union Home Minister to write to the state governments with reference to the above MHA letter that its paragraph regarding "withdrawal" of portions containing references to the Shah Commission Report from the NPC reports by itself be treated as "cancelled and withdrawn," under order of Home Minister Indrajit Gupta.

Having been one of the initiators for basic police reforms measures, starting with the formation of the NPC in 1977 and virtual silence of the governments at the centre and in the states, I used to periodically discuss with Home Minister the imperatives for such reforms from the point of view of the common citizens. During one such discussion towards the end of 1996, the HM wanted me to go through the MHA files on this subject and give him a note as to what steps could be taken by him. Accordingly, he sent a note to the Home Secretary to make available to me within the next 10-15 days all the MHA files on NPC to enable me to prepare my note for the HM.

Instead of the stipulated two weeks, nearly six weeks passed by without even a single file on the subject being sent to me. When the HM enquired after about a month as to the position of the proposed note of mine, I mentioned to him that till then not a single MHA file on the NPC reports had been made available to me despite HM's note to the Home Secretary. It did not take Indrajit Gupta long to fathom why the MHA officers were not reacting promptly and constructively. Hence, he rang up the Home Secretary, asking him to come to HM's room urgently. When he did so, the HM wanted to know why the MHA files on NPC reports were not sent to me as ordered by him even after the lapse of nearly two months.

The Home Secretary was obviously taken aback and responded by saying that the search for the files was continuing but in all probability the files might have been destroyed. Since I was with the HM when the above statement was made by the Home Secretary, I had to intervene by stating that the HM may not be aware of the fact that there were certain categories of government files, whether in the Central Government or in the state governments, which were to be treated as "permanent documents," to be preserved for posterity and eventually deposited with the archives, and that not even the ministers could order their destruction. Hence, the Home Secretary may like to inform the HM as to who was responsible for ordering their destruction so that the HM may decide about the course of action to be taken against the person or persons responsible for 'misplacement' or 'destruction' of such 'permanent' records. The Home Secretary promised the HM his personal intervention in this matter and wanted another seven days to ascertain the 'final' position. The bluff had obviously been called and one slender file was eventually sent to me. It did not take me long thereafter to identify the other connected files and finally about six to eight other fat files concerning the NPC reports surfaced.

While I was busy preparing the Note for the HM on matters relating to follow-up actions by the MHA, a PIL [Writ Petition (Civil) No 316 of 1996: Prakash Singh and others vs Union of India and others] had been filed in the Supreme Court by Prakash Singh, a highly reputed and retired IPS officer, seeking the Court's intervention in the matter of implementation of the basic recommendations of the NPC (1977-82). When the SC wanted to know from the Government of India about steps taken by them till then towards implementation of the NPC recommendations, the game of filibustering started again. The Court was informed through an affidavit filed by the MHA that, as far as the MHA was concerned, the recommendations had been largely acted upon – a totally untrue assertion! When this was brought to the notice of the HM and it transpired that the affidavit on such a vital issue was not even shown to the HM, he ordered its immediate withdrawal and submission of a fresh affidavit only after getting it approved by him.

After receiving my detailed note on the recommendations of the NPC and actions to be taken by the HM/MHA, especially on a priority basis for the basic reforms and restructuring of police including the required changes in the laws governing police, another round of discussion between me and the HM took place. Since most of the implementation part had to be taken by the state governments, the draft of a letter from the HM to the Chief Ministers of states was also given to him by me. Thus emanated the historic semi-official letter dated April 3, 1997 along with a note from the HM appended to the letter.[11]

In view of the continuing relevance of both police reforms and HM's DO letter to the Chief Ministers, some portions of the letter are quoted below:

"... The popular perception all over the country appears to be that many of the deficiencies in the functioning of the police in our country have arisen largely due to an overdose of unhealthy and petty political interference at various levels starting from transfer and posting of policemen of different ranks, misuse of police for partisan purposes and political patronage quite often extended to corrupt police personnel...

"... At the same time, it should be recognised by us that quite often it is the police including the para military forces which have stood between lawlessness verging on anarchy and functioning of our democracy. It is also a fact that, besides the Armed Forces, it is the police and the Central para-military organisations... whose personnel are laying down their lives in our continuing battle against the secessionist and terrorist forces in various parts of our country...

"It is a sad commentary on our professed commitment to the people to provide them with a professionally competent and reasonably clean police administration that we have so far not even made any serious attempt to implement many of the salutary recommendations of the National Police Commission... On the contrary, quite often the recommendations ... have been misrepresented, perhaps deliberately, as amounting to giving unbridled power to the police. In reality, however, proper implementation of the recommendations will amount to not only curbing many of the existing powers of misuse by police but also by those who are the existing controllers of the police, viz., the political executives and the bureaucracy... (These steps) will also ensure greater transparency, accountability and responsiveness to public criticism of police functioning..."

And then Indrajit Gupta's anguished but prophetic concluding remarks

"If recent developments are any indication, judicial intervention in bringing to book many of the allegedly corrupt politicians and other public servants has been hailed by a wide cross section of the people as a step in the right direction. I have a feeling that if the political executives do not take the desired measures even now to bring about the suggested reforms and restructuring of the police, the day may not be far off when the judiciary may intervene decisively to force such socially desirable changes down the throat of the political executives..."

Supreme Court's intervention and perfunctory response of the Centre and the States

The above prophetic warning and voice of sanity of the former Home Minister late Indrajit Gupta went unheeded for nearly ten years but finally led to a categorical directive/order of the Supreme Court on September 22, 2006 in the Prakash Singh PIL. The 11 page landmark judgement of the Supreme Court mandated the following seven items as prelude to other aspects of police reforms:

1 Formation of State Security Commission[12], with the Chief Minister as its chairman and six others as members. It will lay down broad policy guidelines for the functioning of the police and periodically evaluate the performance of the police.

2 Selection procedure of the chief of the State Police (Director General of Police) and his fixed minimum tenure.

3 Minimum tenure also for the IG of Police and some other field officers including the SPs of the districts and the OCs/SHOs of police stations.

4 Separation of the Investigation function from the Law and Order function of police.

5 Setting up of a Police Establishment Board.

6 Setting up of a Police Complaints Authority, and

7 Formation of a National Security Commission.

The Supreme Court further mandated that "The aforesaid directions shall be complied with by the Central Government, State Governments and Union Territories... on or before 31st December, 2006 so that the bodies afore-noted became operational on the onset of the new year..."

Only a few states have complied and that too in a fragmented and perfunctory manner or by diluting the basic thrust of the Supreme Court's directions. The main reasons behind such reluctance are that a professionally independent and truly accountable community centric police may, in the perception of most political masters, seriously jeopardize their control over the anti-social and criminal elements who continue to thrive under their protective umbrella. We can only hope that the younger, and hopefully forward-looking, new generation in police and public life would take courage in both hands and usher in a community centric, professionally competent and cleaner police untainted by political and bureaucratic self-serving interests.

Unified Command and Naga Peace Talks

During HM's visit to J&K and feedback from the officers of various security organisations, including the Army officers operating there as well as in the states in North-East, it was becoming increasingly clear that an unhealthy level of turf war between them was much in evidence which was obviously detrimental to the basic purpose for which they were deployed there. In J&K, for instance, an ex-Army chief was the Governor who, according to army officers posted there, even senior commanders, Lt Generals and Major Generals, used to be treated by him like Majors and Colonels, leading to considerable loss of morale and operational efficiency.

To make matters worse, the Army was insisting that the BSF and the CRPF in J&K should be placed under their command and control, leading to considerable resentment among BSF and CRPF commanders including their respective Directors General. On top of this, the ministers and officers, police as well as civil, of the respective state governments were often treated as if they were only to cater to the demands of all these central forces. A couple of chief ministers also complained of the cavalier fashion in which some of them were often treated.

When all these discordant bits and pieces were put together, an obviously disturbing picture emerged. And that too in respect of matters which were bound to have serious deleterious implications on our national security scenario in the most sensitive areas of our country - be it in J&K or the north-eastern states. During one of my usual informal discussions with the HM in his Western Court office, I brought out all my anxieties in the light of the facts and circumstances mentioned above. In his usual Socratic style, the HM put across some probing questions, gave his own views on some of the above issues and finally asked me: "How would you like this imbroglio to be resolved?"

I responded by stating that it was a more complex issue than what I had initially presumed. I mentioned to him that I had, at the back of my mind, the brief outlines of some institutional mechanism but I would prefer to have these tested during my proposed discussions, on a one-on-one basis and that too separately, with the Home Secretary, Directors General of the BSF, the CRPF and the ITBP besides the Director, IB. "And then only I may get back to you, perhaps for a formal meeting and discussion to be chaired by you and attended by all the above officers.

This would need to be followed up thereafter by informal discussions with representatives of some of the state governments, notably of J&K, Assam, Nagaland and Manipur, and at an appropriate time, we would also consult some critical representatives of the Army, e.g., the Director General of Military Operations/DGMO and the DG, Assam Rifles". The battalions of the Assam Rifles were army units but for administrative purposes, these were placed at the disposal of the Home Ministry for its deployment in the north-eastern states.

During my separate informal discussions with the above officers over the next month or so, it was apparent that –

(a) there was lack of coordination among the security forces as also the absence of mutual understanding of their respective roles;

(b) the state government agencies and the senior functionaries of the government were seldom consulted in advance about force deployment and also about details of the results of operations by the security forces, and more so in respect of the army deployments and operations and results thereof ;

(c) there was hardly any effective sharing of intelligence inputs from their crucial field level intelligence units and hardly any effort at coordination among them.

The Kargil War in the summer 1999 can be treated as a classic example of not so much the lack of intelligence or the lack of coordination among intelligence agencies but lack of serious application of mind and suitable assessment at higher commands including the Army HQ. Almost since August 1997 till about May 1999, there was a fairly steady stream of intelligence inputs from the RAW, IB, BSF and the Field Intelligence Units of the Army. But one is left aghast at the culpable failure on the part of higher army commands to put together the available inputs and the required follow-up measures. A few illustrations, quoted from the Kargil Review Committee Report (KRCR) will depict the state of ineptitude of the higher commands.

The Committee consisted of K Subramaniam as its Chairman and three other members. The Report was submitted to the Government of India on December

15, 1999. Some facts culled out of the above report, as noted below, will reveal the gross failure of the higher commands of the Army over a period of nearly three years despite unbelievably clear intelligence inputs:

- **August 1997:** Presence of Pakistanis in Yaldor sector noticed and reported by the Brigade Intelligence Team (BIT) of 121 Infantry Brigade; the same source (the "Shepherd") also detected Pakistani intrusion on May 3, 1999; all these were 'in the knowledge of the 3 Infantry Division, 15 Corps and the Northern Command' (page 95 of the above Report);
- **June 1998 report of the IB:** (a) "Increased activities at the borders and continuing endeavours to infiltrate a large number of foreign mercenaries in the aftermath of the nuclear tests"; (b) "According to a report from Kargil, increased movement of Pak Army is discernible in Chor, Hadi, Saddle, Reshma, Dhalan and Langar posts along the LoC in the past five days. Pak Army constructing suspension bridge at Khol on river Indus (MRE - 76 degree 13 , N - 34 degree 47, Map No 52B) and a helipad on the bank of river Indus at MRE - 75 degree 49; N-34 degree 39, Map No. 52N)"; (c) "Movement of Pak fighter aircraft at Skardu airstrip". "This report issued by the Directorate of Intelligence Bureau (DIB), while not copied to RAW or JIC/NSCS, was sent to the main consumer, i.e., Directorate General of Military Operation (DGMO) as well as to the Prime Minister, Home Minister, Cabinet Secretary, Home Secretary and Defence Secretary..." Assessment/Action Taken: "These increased activities were part of a heightened alert and activity all along the border

after the nuclear blasts and were in conformity with those". (p. 96, KRCR). What a clumsy assessment by the Army!

- **July 1998:** IB reports: (a) Deployment of M-11 Chinese missiles at Deosal plains (also received by 3 Infantry Division in October 1998); (b) Laying of mines by Pak army near LoC in Kargil sector (also received by 3 Infantry Division in September 1998); (c) infiltration of 30 militants from Kargil border to Doda.
- RAW reported (a) Deployment of 164 Mortar Regiment in Gultari with its detachments deployed along LoC opposite Dras/Kargil sector; (b) 8 Northern Light Infantry (NLI) Battalion deployed in Hamzigund; (c) 69 Baluch deployed at Olthingthang.
- Brigade Intelligence Team (BIT) reported (a) continuous dumping of ammunition and ration.
- **August 1998:** IB reports: (a) Pak Army had been constructing a new post and fortifying defences and bunkers in its territory opposite our post at Chorbat La since July 21, 1998; (b) Pak Army had deployed seven artillery guns and 25 Army personnel at the new post;
- **BIT:** (a) Mixed group of Pak and Afghan militants (30-35) were present at Marol with local guides to cross over to India, (b) Ammunition dumping at all forward areas.
- Similar specific intelligence from IB/RAW/BIT, etc. in September 1998, October 1998, November 1998, December 1998, January to May, 1999.

- A BSF report of December 1998 mentioned that "Fighter aircraft landing every second/third day at Skardu and were also carrying out night practices" + "a new helipad had been made at Deosal opposite our Kaksar area where big size helicopters had been landing, " and so on , vide pp. 95-120 of the KRC Report of December 1999.

In conclusion, one can only feel dismayed that just because of the professional ineptitude and gross negligence of the higher commands, a large body of our brave and young officers and jawans had to pay the ultimate price with their lives during the Kargil War. And we are as yet unaware if some of these guilty officers were at all punished for their demonstrably culpable negligence and professional incompetence or such officers were promoted 'in due course'!

It also transpired during my personal interactions and inquiries that the chief ministers/ home ministers of most such states seldom bothered to make their presence felt even in vital matters of national security or even security of their own states. Under law, the armed forces of the Union are deployed in a state "in aid of the civil authorities" but the burden of responsibility of the state governments cannot be ignored. But the impression was inescapable that most chief ministers were 'playing safe' so as not to invite the pointed wrath of insurgent/ terrorist groups!

In the light of the above facts and circumstances, I held further detailed discussions with the Home Minister and suggested that it was high time that the loosely articulated and interpreted provisions of law, perhaps to evade responsibility, may have to be brought within the framework of some institutional mechanism with clear-cut roles and responsibilities at all levels. Obviously, the HM had no hesitation in agreeing with my views and asked me to work out the details of such a mechanism.

On receiving his endorsement in principle, we set about detailed discussions on a number of occasions with the Home Secretary, chiefs of the major Central Police Organisations (BSF/CRPF/ITBP/ etc.) and also with the Director, Intelligence Bureau and a few others including the Army's Director General of Military Operations (DGMO) and Director General of Military Intelligence (DGMI). The views of the crucial states' chief secretaries and DGPs were duly elicited. The HM also consulted the chief ministers of the concerned states (J&K, Manipur, Nagaland, Tripura, Assam, etc.). The PMO and the Cabinet Secretary were also involved during the consultation process.

What emerged out of such high-level consultations was the basic structures and the institutional mechanism called 'Unified Command' (UC) for each of the insurgency/terrorism-affected states, especially for J&K and some of the states of the north-east. Briefly stated, the basic objective of the UC was to apportion specific responsibility, geographical as well as operational, for each of the following three tiers as indicated below:

(a) State HQ level UC for overall policy, planning, coordination and monitoring of the activities of the other levels. This state-level apex UC was to be headed by the CM of the state and comprising of the state's Chief Secretary and the Director General of Police and the senior most officers of the Army, Assam Rifles, BSF, CRPF and other central police and intelligence agencies. This apex body was to meet at least once a month, take stock of the prevailing situation, apportion tasks to the agencies concerned and finally, to monitor the results so that necessary modifications could be made, both for planning and operational aspects of the counter-insurgency measures.

(b) The second tier was the regional/zonal UCs, covering two or three districts or such other geographical area as was considered necessary. Its composition was largely on the pattern of the apex UC, except that these were to be headed by the senior most officer of the Army/Assam Rifles or other central forces having the maximum force presence in the region. Its tasks were, *mutatis mutandis,* on the pattern of the apex UC and should continue to be under the overall supervisory control of the latter.

(c) The third tier – Area UCs were patterned on the regional UCs and with similar composition. These Area UCs were to be the real cutting edge of the entire scheme. Their jurisdictions were to be clearly demarcated on maps, after mutual consultations among its members. It was the responsibility of these Area UCs to plan and organise operations in their respective areas, except when they felt that the higher formations needed to be consulted in view of its ramifications in other areas. These Area UCs were also required to carry out operations on the basis of larger planning by the Regional/Zonal UCs. It goes without saying that the state's zonal/regional officers also to be treated as a part of the regional or area UCs and were to be consulted/co-opted as far as possible because their local knowledge and information could prove to be of considerable value in planning and executing such operations.

As far as my knowledge goes, the above scheme was put into practice at all the above three levels and in most of the states mentioned earlier (i.e. J&K, Nagaland, Manipur, Assam and Tripura in particular) during the later part of 1996 and continued without any hitch at least till early 1998. I am not in a position to state categorically what happened thereafter or what is its fate now.

Beginning of the Naga Peace Process

According to many experts, the epicenter of the separatist politics as also of insurgency in the northeastern states was Nagaland. Almost since the early years after India's independence on August 15, 1947, AZ Phizo, with the suspected patronage of Rev. Michael Scott started organising the Naga rebellion under the umbrella of his organisation known as the Naga National Council (NNC). The insurgents had no dearth of funds and were not slow in acquiring arms from across the amorphous and virtually unmanned Burma border.

With the escalating levels of violence even against dissident Naga tribes and groups, the Government of India took the first decisive step by substantial deployment of its security forces to curb the lawlessness and violence unleashed by Phizo's NNC activists. Eventually in 1972, the NNC was declared as a banned organisation, forcing Phizo to shift his base to London where he died later.

Patricia Mukhim[13], an eminent journalist and social activist belonging to the north-east brings out the basics of the Naga imbroglio thus: "To understand the internal dynamics of Nagaland, it is important to understand the Naga identity. But is there such a thing as Naga identity? Prior to the British Colonial Rule, the concept of

Nagaland was fluid. The area was inhabited by groups of people of the Tibeto-Burman origin. But there is no historical evidence that these were one people with a common culture. Hence, the deep-rooted tribalism or tribe and clan loyalty that asserts itself even today. Intra-tribe warfare and killings and head hunting was part and parcel of the so called Naga people before the advent of Christianity. When the tribes converted, religion brought a sobering effect on them. Intra-tribal feuds lessened but Christianity failed to channelise the militant traits of the people they converted into more positive, creative outlets… " Patricia Mukhim continues further to state that in her interactions with a large number of Naga people in different areas, she "noticed their difficulties in internalising the 'Naga' identity and allowing that to subsume their tribal identity. An Angami is proud of his tribal heritage and will defend it to hilt. So will a Sema or an Ao…"

Before we turn to the historic Naga peace process, especially the 'ceasefire' agreement between the major Naga insurgent group, namely, NSCN (IM) and the Government of India spearheaded by the Home Ministry in 1997 under Home Minister Indrajit Gupta's support, it is necessary to understand the inner conflicts among the Naga tribes. Thus, according to a perceptive Angami Naga scholar Charles Chasie, most of the disparate tribes have different cultures, social practices and political system: Konyaks, Semas and Tankhuls have a form of autocratic rule. The Ao people have a more enlightened structure; they have village councils that affiliate themselves to an apex body. Angamis, on the other hand, appeared more democratic since they search for a consensus on any issue.[14]

In terms of its numerical superiority, stock of arms and violence potential, the Naga insurgent group known as the NSCN (IM), led by Isac Chasie and Thuingling Muivah, was at the forefront. Paradoxically, its principal leader Muivah was not a resident of Nagaland proper but belonged to the Tangkhul Naga tribe of Ukhrul district in the hilly terrain of the neighbouring state of Manipur. The other active insurgent group, known as NSCN(K), was led by Khaplang, having its principal base in Myanmar region bordering India.

We all know that AZ Phizo, founder of the Naga National Council (NNC), died in London, a forlorn and disillusioned person and thereafter his daughter Adino Phizo proclaimed herself as the president of the NNC and continued to live in London, almost without any root or support base in Nagaland. However, during a recent interview[15], she spewed venom against Muivah and his NSCN(IM): "...In the affairs of Nagaland, Th Muivah is a non-entity. He is from Ukhrul district in Manipur and has no political roots in Nagaland... On the question of the so called NSCN(IM), its blood-thirsty origin in 1979-80 and its persistent lies and hatred campaign to subvert the Yehzabo (constitution) of Nagaland has been a hideous distraction... Over the past three decades, the people of Nagaland have endured extreme violence at the hands of the outfit, generally called tormentors..."

By the time Indrajit Gupta assumed charge as the Union Home Minister in July 1996, the Nagaland imbroglio was bound to be one of his important tasks at hand besides Kashmir and the Assam-Bodo violent skirmishes. His totally non-partisan and innovative approaches, on top of his well-known and all-round political credibility, soon started having its impact through a discernible thaw in violence in all the known epicenters of persistent violence - J&K, Nagaland, Manipur and Assam. We have already mentioned about the Unified Command mechanism introduced in all the above regions, which too started having the expected impact in all these states with a lessening in the scale, intensity and frequency of violence.

Persisting menace of extortion by underground insurgent groups

However, the menace of extortion by virtually all the underground insurgent groups in the affected states in the north-east were known to be widespread and no political leaders including ministers dared to take any firm step. On the contrary, quite a few of them were known to be the shareholders of such extortion rackets !

Another common 'disease' afflicting almost all these states was the widespread corruption indulged in by most of the ministers, duly aided by their henchmen contractors and quietly abetted by groups of officers. All the money thus 'looted' was the vast amount of central funds, because hardly any of these states had been discharging their constitutional, legal and administrative responsibility of their respective state's revenue collection!

Quite often I was a sad witness to these ministers coming to meet the Home Minister in Delhi, primarily to request for more 'generous' allotment of central funds. Indrajit Gupta being what he was, quite often could not desist from chastising them thus:

"Mr Chief Minister/Minister, can you please send me a statement showing how much revenue collection on various prescribed heads could be done by your government during the past two years and, secondly, what was the net outcome of the central funds during the same period?" Like his proverbial 'sting in the tail', Indrajit Gupta at times could not resist the temptation of sounding a veiled threat: "Mr Chief Minister/Minister, please do not think that we all in the Home Ministry are so naïve as not to have some credible information about the cosy relationship between some politicians, contractors and officers for siphoning off most of the central funds!"[16]

Such anguished outbursts by Indrajit Gupta, perhaps were the first of its kind in the history of the Home Ministry. But, alas, their long-term impact could well be guessed, faced as we were (and perhaps still are) with bunches of greedy, selfish, shameless and rapacious political leaders, aided and abetted by an equally self-seeking bureaucracy! And unfortunately for us, this spectacle is not confined to those states only - the recent 2G spectrum scam at the central level and that too of mind-boggling amounts of money, is a continuing tragedy and shame of the Indian democracy!

The NSCN(IM) being the most potent and organised insurgent group causing needless death and destruction in the region, the Government of India had started, through the Home Ministry at least since early 1990s, some 'informal'(track-2 ?) contacts continued with the leaders of the organisation, both within and outside India. Finally, the ice was broken around mid-1997, thanks to the sustained efforts of some officers backed by Indrajit Gupta. The HM's credibility and clout in the Government also influenced the NSCN (IM) leadership. Thus, as against their earlier stand that any dialogue for a mutually acceptable peace process will have to take place in some other country outside India, Indrajit Gupta's firm stand that this will have to be in Delhi itself, though with a clear and unequivocal undertaking by the HM that none of its emissaries for talks will be detained or arrested or even harassed. Surprisingly and much to our relief, the NSCN (IM) agreed to the above proposition of the HM. A large part of the credit for this goes to our track-2 officers, even though the HM and I were in regular touch with these officers and did our best to smoothen the rough edges and overcome any hurdle in their painstaking and sustained efforts.

Finally the 'peace talks' with NSCN (IM)

The actual 'talks' took place on 7th and 8th November, 1997 in a quiet place ('safe house') in South Delhi area where arrangements were made for accommodating the NSCN representatives from 6th onwards. The ground rules for the proposed 'cease fire' agreement, as worked out by the Home Secretary and the DIB were finalised a few days in advance in a meeting with the HM. Prior to that, the MHA officers also had consultations with representatives of the Army (HQ Eastern Command/3 Corps HQ/ Military Operations Directorate of the Army HQ). Likewise, the BSF and CRPF chiefs were also consulted.

As desired by the HM, I accompanied the MHA delegation comprising Home Secretary, K Padmanabhaiah, DIB, Arun Bhagat, and a few others in the afternoon of 7th November 1997 to the house selected for the meetings with the Naga delegation. The NSCN (IM) team consisted of five persons: VS Atem, aged about 45 years and leader of the Naga delegation, their SS and C-in-C, AK Lungalang, aged about 65 years – another SS and a 'minister'; Jamie Lotha, aged about 40 years and their Area Organiser ; Pungthang Simrah, aged about 30 years and a Battalion Commander; the fifth person whose name I can't recall, was aged about 30 years and was, surprisingly, a contractor from Manipur and a nephew of Muivah.

The introductory discussions with the Naga delegation started on the 7th November itself around 7.30 pm. The talks were resumed the next day on 8th November around 11 am. The HM and I were closeted in HM's North Block office for periodical feedback from one of the IB officers attending the talks about the progress in this crucial discussions. Around 12.30 hours, the DIB, one of our important interlocutors attending the talks, rang me up from the meeting place to say that the Naga delegation had taken serious exception to certain 'rude' remarks by the Home Secretary (leader of the MHA delegation) and that they were about to walk out in protest! Sensing that this would have disastrous and long-term consequences, after all the preparatory work by us all on both sides. Hence, after a hurried consultation with the HM, I requested the DIB to inform both sides that an emissary of the Home Minister would visit them shortly, with suitable message from the HM and also further requested the DIB to inform both sides accordingly as also to ensure that both the delegation members remain in the building. The HM desired that I should visit the venue urgently once again and try my best to avert any collapse of the dialogue process.

How an unexpected collapse of the talks could be averted by 'unconventional' method

On reaching the house, I could sense the tension prevailing there and hence had to quickly think out ways for diffusing the tense atmosphere of palpable gloom. First, I had a brief discussion with the MHA delegation and went over to the adjacent room where the Naga delegation was huddled together, obviously in a sullen mood. I had no difficulty in locating Mr Atem, leader of the Naga delegation, introduced myself to him and enquired whether he was a smoker! Obviously, he was somewhat taken aback by my unusual query and replied in the affirmative, with a flicker of smile, on his otherwise inscrutable face. I said that I myself was a 'sinner' and requested him to come out so that both of us could smoke and also have some tea or coffee as he liked. I could feel that the first hurdle was crossed.

Mr Atem was pleasantly surprised at my unusual gesture and we both went over to the adjacent verandah where the two of us could smoke as well as talk informally over cups of coffee. I mentioned to him that the HM was personally upset at the unfortunate turn of events and requested him to forget the unintentional interlude so that both sides could get on with the vital and sensitive discussion for a satisfactory and mutually agreed solution.

At the end of our coffee and smoking session, we embraced each other, shook hands and then I took him back to the negotiation table. The discussions thereafter, which I attended for an hour or so, were cordial and without any further loss of dignity and trust on either side. When I went back to North Block and reported this happy interlude to the Home Minister, he was immensely relieved, thanked me profusely and we both again started looking forward to a satisfactory conclusion of our talks with the Naga delegation.

It is a matter of history now that the final outcome of a mutually agreed 'ceasefire' agreement emerged out of this meeting of 7-8 November 1997, which has been largely sustained and honoured on both sides till now (2012). And this remarkable breakthrough in the decades-long skirmishes and bloodshed between NSCN(IM) and the Indian Security Forces in Nagaland, besides other people in the states of Assam, Manipur and Mizoram was possible largely due to the genuine and unstinting support and advice of the then Union Home Minister Indrajit Gupta. A large part of the credit also goes to the dedicated, untiring and persevering role of the officers of MHA and other intelligence and security agencies. We all owe a debt of gratitude to all of them as also to the Naga delegation members.

References

1 Ranjit Gupta, commonly known as Runu Gupta, retired as an eminent and respected Chief Secretary of the government of West Bengal in the 1960s. I was privileged to have him as the CS when I was a Deputy Commissioner of Police in Calcutta and got to know him and his gracious wife Mira Gupta more closely for many years even after he retired from the service.

2 The UF consisted of CPM, CPI, Forward Block, RSP, Janata Dal, Samajwadi Party, Telugu Desham, Trinamul Congress, AGP, DMK, Congress (Tiwari Group), Maharashtrawadi Gomantak Dal and Republican Party.

3 This room became my temporary residence in Delhi almost till the end of December, 1997 when I had to shift to Mizoram as its Governor on December 28, 1997.

4 In the Bathanitola carnage, a total of 21 dalits were brutally killed including an 8-month old baby and a 80-year old woman. This dastardly act was allegedly perpetrated by

one of the Senas of the landlord class. Even in a case of this magnitude, the verdict by the Additional Sessions Judge was passed as late as on May 6, 2010, holding 23 of the accused persons as guilty and acquitted 30 others 'for lack of sufficient evidence'. It is not known if the sentence had been executed till now.

5 We will have occasion to revert to this aspect later, viz., 'unified command' to be headed by the Chief Minister of the State.

6 I was pleasantly surprised that Peer's personal reflections with telling candour and objectivity resonated with many of my own views about the Kashmir situation, especially in the light of my exposure in Baramula to the true spirit of Kashmiriyaat!

7 Recently, I came across a news item "Come, sow our land, Sudan tells Punjabis: reeling from power crisis and paucity of farm hands - such offer could be a boon for Punjabis," *Times of India,* August 2, 2009. I am quite sure that the enterprising Punjabis would take up this challenge, which would benefit both countries. Why couldn't someone, I wondered, sell the idea of huge tracts of fertile lands in Bulgaria being taken up for proper use by some enterprising farmers of India !

8 Perhaps the situation might have changed for the better after Vladimir Putin assumed power but I really don't know the ground-level reality then.

9 I had known Mr Saksena earlier too when he was the DIG of Delhi Police of which my father-in-law BB Banerji (IP/1934/Bihar cadre) was the Inspector General of Delhi Police during 1960-65.

10 The members of the newly set up NPC were NK Reddy, a former Judge of Madras High Court; KF Rustamji, ex-IGP, Madhya Pradesh, first DG of BSF and ex-Special Secretary, Home Ministry; NS Saksena, ex-IGP, UP and ex-DG, CRPF and then Member, UPSC; Prof MS Gore,

Professor Tata Institute of Social Sciences, Bombay and CV Narasimhan, a former Director, CBI as the full-time Member-Secretary of the Commission. The government notification No. VI-24021/36/77-GPA.I dated November 15, 1977 to that effect was issued by the Ministry of Home Affairs, Government of India, containing 15 terms of reference for the Commission.

11 It was learnt later that this letter along with the Note formed part of the records of the Supreme Court in the PIL case referred to earlier.

12 In HM's DO letter a modified nomenclature as Police Control Authority was suggested. It may be mentioned here that the Second Administrative Reforms Commission of India (August, 2005 - April 2009) provided an even more explicit name - Police Performance & Accountability Commission.

13 Patricia Mary Mukhim, "*North-East Scan*," Dialogue Quarterly, April-June 2005, pp. 11-20.

14 Op. cit., p. 14.

15 Interview from her London residence of Adino Phizo by Oken Jeet Sandham, Editor of *North-East Herald* and published in The Statesman (Calcutta) of 28th June, 2010, p. 8.

Chapter 4

Concluding Observations

Growing Dimensions of Corruption in India

While having a relook at my above observations on three of the well-known and outstanding personalities, viz., Jyoti Basu, Rajiv Gandhi and Indrajit Gupta, I must admit that in the context of present-day India, the one glaring malaise afflicting our country as also our polity, is the all-pervasive corruption which make all self-respecting Indians hang their heads in shame. How I wish we had in our midst now the suave but firm administrator like Jyoti Basu, an equally suave and modern man like Rajiv Gandhi, and the tough and straight-talking Indrajit Gupta. A combination like the above, alas, is too good to be true in the current murky politico-administrative atmosphere!

This cancerous growth of corruption in our body politic, be it in the arena of politics and governance or in the spheres of day-to-day administration from the highest to the lowest levers of power—from the Central and state administrations down to the panchayat levels - must be a cause for serious concern for all self-respecting Indians. So is the case with nearly unchecked corruption in the corporate sector. SS Gill says "Our archaic legal system is not only least suited to the promotion of a democratic, egalitarian, welfare state, it fosters an outlook which is subversive to social equity and the provisions of the Directive Principles of the Constitution. The focal point of colonial justice was the individual and protection of private property rights. On the other hand, the emphasis of a welfare state is on the rights of the society and social justice.

Hence, our legal system undermines the societal goals. Whereas, a starving person is jailed for a minor theft, a millionaire who steals crores of public money by evading mandatory taxes is treated with kid gloves and let off with a fine. Unscrupulous businessmen and traders who extensively adulterate food items and produce spurious drugs, thus damaging the health of millions, get away with impunity. Industrialists ravage the environment by toxic wastes of their factories and still go scot-free. Even the courts have not gone beyond giving directions for the relocation of the polluting industries. In short, the social dimension of law is very weak and private interest gets precedence over social good"[1].

"The existing legal system has inbuilt provisions for delays," continues SS Gill, "prolonged litigation and evasion. Its provisions are ideally suited to the promotion of corruption at all levels, as graft provides the quickest immunity from delays and punitive action....

"Another significant development was the emergence of a politician-bureaucrat nexus at the district level [2]..."A few illustrations from the 'eminent gallery of rogues'

T Prakasam Episode

The above exposition of Gill, unexceptionable though, does not adequately bring out the social, historical and national psyche of a people who so easily give into the temptation of the gains of corrupt practices. Let us go back in history. T Prakasam was a tall freedom fighter from Madras, Tamil Nadu, who worked along with Gandhi, Nehru and Sardar Patel. It was reported in the Press that during his tours in his state in 1945, several purses filled with money were presented to him at public functions, which he treated as his personal property! Coming to know of it, Gandhi was very annoyed and wrote so in his journal *The Harijan* and 'decried the practice of presenting purses to Congressmen'.

Fullstop, as far as Gandhiji was concerned! However, Sardar Patel wrote directly to Prakasam 'to verify facts'. Prakasam unashamedly offered a truly astounding defence. He argued that the purses were presented to him by his followers and admirers 'as compensation for the losses he had sustained owing to his participation in the freedom struggle'. Patel insisted that the money was collected from poor peasants and must be passed on to Congress Committee. Prakasam persisted with his defence and came up with a brazen-faced proposition that the purses were a 'legitimate means of financing political workers'. It was only after a 'reprimand' from Gandhi that Prakasam relented and parted with his hoard.

It is most unfortunate that this trend seems to have persisted with many politicians even down to the present era: Thus two successive Telecom ministers at the centre, both from Tamil Nadu, are widely believed to have looted thousands of crores of public fund without the slightest sense of shame. Incidentally, one of them had to be sent to jail, now on bail after about a year, and still facing criminal charges in a court of law. However, it is anybody's guess as to when the trial will commence or end and with what result!

Haridas Mundhra-T T Krishnamachari Saga

In view of persisting complaints of corruption in high places, the Government appointed the Santhanam Committee in 1962 to examine the issue in detail and suggest remedial measures. The Committee submitted its report in 1964 and no earth-shaking steps were either suggested by the Committee or taken by the Government. As a result, skeletons were tumbling out of the closets at fairly regular intervals: the Haridas Mundhra-TT Krishnamachari (Finance Minister) episode of LIC scandal, which finally led to Krishnamachari's resignation in the wake of Justice MC Chagla Inquiry Commission Report.

Serajuddin – KD Malaviya episode and Sardar Pratap Singh Kairon saga

Then followed the Serajuddin-KD Malaviya, Minister of Mines and Fuel, scandal in 1963 which rocked the Parliament and eventually Malaviya had to resign. And then came the turn of the Punjab strongman and its Chief Minister Pratap Singh Kairon. When he became Chief Minister in 1956, he owned a few acres of land and his wife had to work as a school teacher to augment family income. As the Chief Minister he allowed his wife and son Surender Singh and other relatives to acquire substantial wealth, in various forms; cinema houses, plots of land, etc. by abusing his official patronage. Initially, for a couple of years, Jawaharlal Nehru as Prime Minister did not give any importance to even written complaints by MPs and others. Eventually, a public interest petition was filed in the Supreme Court, whereupon the President advised the Prime Minister to order a regular inquiry. Then only the PM set up in November 1963, a Commission of Inquiry by the retired Chief Justice of India, Justice SR Das, a person of impeccable reputation for his integrity.

On the basis of evidence on record, the SR Das Commission concluded that several of the charges against Kairon were proved. Its report was submitted on June 11, 1964, a fortnight after Nehru's death. His successor Lal Bahadur Shastri initially refused to publish the report. But later, on strong public demand, he advised Kairon to step down. When Kairon refused to do so, Shastri released the report. Thereafter, Kairon had no option but to resign.

Another 'roll of dishonour': Bakshi Ghulam Mohammed

Similar was the case with another chief minister – Bakshi Ghulam Mohammed of Jammu and Kashmir who succeeded Sheikh Mohammed Abdullah when the latter was arrested after a coup in 1953. Bakshi ruled the state for the next ten years as his personal fiefdom. Reports and representations against his high-handedness and corruption started pouring in right from the beginning. In this case, as in the case of Kairon, Nehru persisted in disbelieving the allegations and ignored them.

Nehru perhaps thought that to keep the National Conference in power and defeat the designs of the Pakistan-aided secessionists, a strongman like Bakshi was necessary. But he did not realise that Bakshi was fully exploiting this state of affairs, and was making hay while the sun shone and was looting the state and the people of Jammu and Kashmir. Finally, Nehru eased him out under the garb of the Kamaraj Plan in October 1963.

Bakshi's successor GM Sadiq appointed in January 1965 a Commission of Inquiry, Justice NR Ayyangar Commission, to look into the allegations of corruption against the former Chief Minister Bakshi Ghulam Mohammed. The Commission submitted its report in June 1967. This report revealed that Bakshi came from a family of tailors with very modest means and that he himself was working as a salesman of Khadi Bhandar on a salary of Rs. 20 per month. Then he embarked on his political career which eventually catapulted him to the office of the chief minister.

The inquiry report further revealed that during his fairly long tenure as the chief minister, he along with his five brothers and numerous other relatives went on a money-making spree in a most blatant manner. They acquired various agencies, cinema houses, petrol pumps and other movable and immovable properties by abusing his official position in a crude and blatant manner. The Ayyangar Commission estimated the value of the family's known assets as Rs 34 lakh, estimated value in 1997 was Rs 7 crore, according to SS Gill[3].

Jawaharlal Nehru's Era

Jawaharlal Nehru himself was considered by all his contemporaries as 'the cleanest of politicians', even while in power as the all powerful Prime Minister of India. When he learnt that some of his trusted ministers were resorting to unethical or corrupt practices, his initial reaction was that these were not true, and that was his as also the country's greatest misfortune. But when he learnt that his ancestral house in Allahabad, Anand Bhawan was assessed to an unusually low rate of property tax, he protested and had the amount raised by 500 per cent. Likewise, on his seventieth birthday, GD Birla, the noted industrialist, sent him a cheque for Rs. 70, 000, with a request to spend the amount for any public purpose he liked. And Nehru's response: he had the cheque returned to Birla immediately! But when it came to taking firm steps against his corrupt political associates, he could not be decisive, because he could never believe that his associates, ministers or others, could ever stoop so low as to indulge in corrupt practices, and that was his greatest weakness.

And this mental block prevented him from agreeing to the setting up of a permanent tribunal to hold inquiries against his ministers, even in the face of the President's suggestion to appoint a 'high powered, independent tribunal to inquire into and, if necessary, to initiate investigations into charges against people in high positions'. Incidentally, this is akin to the recent controversy about the government's Lokpal Bill and the Anna Hazare team's Jan Lokpal Bill, and this controversy is yet to be resolved in a conclusive manner.

Corruption and Indira Gandhi regime

"Whereas Nehru had all along resisted the demand for creating a permanent agency to inquire into bribery charges against ministers, Indira Gandhi, while presiding over the Congress Working Committee meeting in New Delhi on 30-31 December 1959, herself proposed the setting up of special committees or tribunals which would look into complaints of misconduct against persons in authority. She was emphatic that the people should not get the impression that those in high positions could get away with anything[4]".

It is wellknown that Indira Gandhi's own lifestyle was austere and that she was a person of frugal habits; like her father, she was not acquisitive, and money in itself had no attraction for her. "But unlike him, she well understood the temptation and allure money had for most people... and a penchant for realpolitik which led her to shed her earlier inhibitions about political corruption, exploiting instead its full potential as a tool for gaining and retaining power.... If the way to hell is paved with good intentions, Indira Gandhi's introduction of the 'licence-quota-permit raj' confirms it to the hilt. It was in genuine pursuit of socialist goals that Indira tried to regulate and control economic activity in the private sector. It was to achieve these goals that she enacted the Monopolies and Restrictive Trade Practices (MRTP) Act in 1970, and the Foreign Exchange Regulation Act (FERA) in 1973. She also modified taxation policies with a view to reducing income disparities and mobilizing higher resources for the Plans[5]".

"These well-intentioned measures represent a landmark in the spread of administrative and political corruption in India. Henceforth licences, permits and clearances had to be obtained for setting up new industries, expanding the capacity of existing ones, import of capital equipment and spares, and release of foreign exchange for all these items. Complete and elaborate export and import regulations were framed to keep a check on the outflow of foreign exchange and penalise those who violated the guidelines[6]".

The regulatory mechanism gave the government extensive powers of patronage and thus emerged fresh avenues of corruption and extortion - by politicians and regulators alike. These provisions also opened the floodgate of corrupt practices by the business and corporate sectors who were obliged to dish out funds not only to official functionaries but also political party operatives. Thus, the floodgate of multi-crore corruption was opened up, much to the delight of everyone.

However, all the above well-intentioned measures led to uncontrolled and widespread avenues of administrative and political corruption, much beyond the capacity of any administration or political leader to eradicate. This would be evident from some of the notable cases referred to below.

Rajiv Gandhi and Corruption

As is well-known, Rajiv Gandhi was the most reluctant entrant into the turmoil of the political arena. It was also a fact that he was a gentleman to the core, perhaps somewhat akin to his grandfather Jawaharlal Nehru and not given to pettiness or political skullduggery. But most regrettably, such traits were taken advantage of by some of his close associates and advisers. Thus his name got unfairly associated with quite a few government deals during his time - the Fairfax contract, HBJ Pipeline contract, the HDW submarine deal as also the Bofors gun purchase deal.

Fairfax and Reliance Industries Affair

As the Prime Minister, he asked his Finance Minister VP Singh to take stern measures against the economic offenders as part of his cleansing campaign. Meanwhile, the Enforcement Directorate under the charge of Bhure Lal, a crusading bureaucrat, had started investigating some of the allegedly shady deals of the Reliance Industries of Dhirubhai Ambani. Around this time, Gurumurthy, an adviser in Ambani rival Ramnath Goenka's newspaper *Indian Express*, emerged on the scene, who suggested to Bhure Lal that it may be better not to depend on any Indian investigating agency in respect of the cases against Dhirubhai Ambani and instead bring in the American Investigative Agency called Fairfax. Surprisingly, Bhure Lal swallowed this bait of Gurumurthy and Fairfax was brought in with the concurrence of the Revenue Secretary Vinod Pande and the Finance Minister VP Singh.

"Dhirubhai, who was keeping a close watch on the progress of investigation against him, was not the one to passively watch his ruination. He launched his counter-offensive in his own style. Suddenly, a letter to Gurumurthy, purported to be written by McKay, vice-president of Fairfax surfaced in the office of Mohan Katre, Director, CBI. This letter revealed that Fairfax had been commissioned by the Finance Ministry to investigate the Swiss properties of Amitabh Bachchan and his foreign associates. It also referred to a fee of $ 500,000 to be paid jointly to Fairfax by Nusli Wadia, head of Bombay Dyeing and Ambani's rival, and RN Goenka, owner of the *Indian Express*. A copy of this letter was also given to Amitabh Bachchan[7]".

Gill continued: "The letter was obviously a crude forgery. Its English was awkward and it was typed on a manual typewriter. And as McKay said, 'To write such a letter would be a stupid thing to do, like putting a gun to your own head'. But stories about investigation against the Bachchan brothers and Rajiv's Italian relations had been circulating for quite sometime, and after this incident

Amitabh became quite jittery. While Katre brought the letter to the PM's notice, Amitabh met Rajiv separately with its copy[8]".

At this stage, let me share with the readers my personal knowledge about the above affair. When Katre was the Director, CBI, I happened to be CBI's Additional Director. Katre used to tell me and others too quite often that his Bombay-based son had been earning quite a lot – "Ten times more than what I (Katre) had been earning," Katre boasted! Once, out of curiosity, I enquired what his son had been doing, and his response was that his son was in some business venture of his own, in which he was assisted by Dhirubhai Ambani! I was not really surprised because it was a fairly common knowledge among CBI officers about Katre's close link with Dhirubhai.

It was also known in CBI circle that Katre was desperately trying to be 'close' to Prime Minister Rajiv Gandhi. Hence, the surfacing of the so called Fairfax (McKay) letter on ***Katre's desk first,*** did not come as a surprise to most of the CBI officers, and it was suspected that the letter itself originated from Dhirubhai's cronies, perhaps at the instance of Katre. However, Dhirubhai's myriad manipulative genius could not be matched by any official agency or officers, and he made his big pile in due course in the Reliance cases.

According to some knowledgeable circles, "The handling of the Fairfax inquiry is the best illustration of Rajiv's inexperience and gullibility. The case had nothing to do with him or his Italian relations. A business tycoon i.e., Dhirubhai Ambani, to save his skin, planted a forged letter and killed three birds with one stone. First, he shook the Enforcement Directorate off his back. Second, he got rid of the Finance Minister and his two crusading officers, viz., Vinod Pande and Bhure Lal, who had become a threat to his business interests. Third, he got an opportunity to get close to the Prime Minister. Ambani achieved all this by playing upon the fears of Amitabh Bachchan who, in turn, planted the conspiracy theory in Rajiv's mind. In this manoeuvre he was greatly assisted by Katre, Director CBI, who was beholden to Ambani for the lucrative business openings he had provided to his son[9]".

Bofors Gun Deal and Rajiv Gandhi

On March 24, 1987 India had signed a contract with Bofors, a sister company of the Nobel Industries (Sweden) for the purchase of four hundred FH-77 howitzers (155-mm) at a cost of $ 1.3 billion (about Rs 1,700 crore). Their competitor was the gun of a French Company called Sofoma, but an expert committee was in favour of the former both in terms of its quality and price. Considering all these facts as also the lower price quoted by Bofors, the Prime Minister's option was in favour of the Bofors guns. But he made it clear that there should be no middlemen, and the Bofors had to accept this stipulation and gave a loosely-worded undertaking to the Ministry of Defence.

Surprisingly, when the contract deal was prepared jointly by Bofors and the Ministry officials, the above stipulation was not included in it. This material omission was not owned by anybody later but it was clear from subsequent revelations that Arun Nehru might have had some role to play in this regard. Later the blame was passed on to the Prime Minister/PMO by the wily bureaucrats and self-seeking army brass, perhaps at the instance of Arun Nehru as was revealed later by which time his relations with Rajiv had been considerably strained.

The inept handling of the whole issue started becoming self-defeating after the sordid revelations in *The Hindu* newspaper by its editor N Ram and journalist Chitra Subramaniam. This was largely the undoing of some of the trusted aides and advisers of Rajiv Gandhi. I would not like to dwell further on this issue and refer the readers to my earlier chapter on Rajiv Gandhi, subtitled 'Bofors Gun Deal' and 'My last meeting with Rajiv Gandhi'.

However, as was revealed and tested on the ground during the critical Kargil War, 1999, everyone including the army brass were full of praise for the quality of the gun. But by then Rajiv's credibility *vis-à-vis* the Bofors issue had been called to question.

Corruption in the post-Nehru-Gandhi era

The era of a stable one-party rule came to an end when the Congress failed to win a majority in the 1989 Lok Sabha poll. Then followed two short spells of coalition governments headed respectively by VP Singh and Chandrashekhar, and the mid-term poll of May-June, 1991. The Congress again failed to win an absolute majority and its last charismatic leader Rajiv Gandhi was assassinated when the elections were still in progress.

Maimed and dispirited, the Congress cobbled up a majority with outside help, and elected the low-profile PV Narasimha Rao as its leader[10]. This was an interim arrangement, because Rao was not even given a Parliamentary ticket owing to his poor health. But the 'tonic of power' soon rejuvenated the old man and he started recovering both his health and his lost political clout!

Around this time in mid-1991, the story about a multi-crore hawala scam surfaced as a sequel to Delhi Police's arrest of one AA Lone of the Kashmir terrorist outfit called Hizbul Mujahideen. Owing to its sensitive nature, the government transferred the case to CBI. However, the Delhi Police had already discovered the conduit through which funds from abroad were being fed to this terrorist group. CBI, in turn, traced the main actors - Mohini Jain in London and Tariq Bhai in Dubai, both of whom used to transfer funds through their hawala channels. During these investigations, the name of Surendra Jain, the elder of the Jain brothers, as the main operator of the hawala scam, surfaced.

CBI investigation revealed that earlier the Jain brothers had paid a bribe of Rs 6.5 crore to the Energy Minister Arif Mohammad Khan for helping them bag some big contracts of the Bhilai Engineering Corporation as also for the Kawas Project in Gujarat. Eventually, the CBI raided in May 1991 the house of one JK Jain, a trusted accountant of the Jain brothers. Besides a lot of cash, the raid also unearthed two diaries and two notebooks, containing entries of numerous payments.

The entries referred to payments made to a large number of top politicians and ministers from time to time. Curiously, CBI did not initially reveal the names of the recipients - perhaps not to alert the recipients of the hawala funds in advance till extensive and simultaneous raids could be organised in various parts of India, especially in and around Delhi. Unfortunately, a CBI officer on deputation from Delhi Police, betrayed the professional trust and leaked out the list of the recipients, and *Jansatta,* a Hindi daily, published the complete list of 115 recipients of the tainted hawala funds.

And Narasimha Rao, the Chanakya of Indian politics, got embroiled in a series of financial scams - some of his own making and in some he helped others in making money. Thus, the multi-crore Jain Hawala scam surfaced - slowly to start with. After the retirement of Justice Venkatachelliah as the Chief Justice of the Supreme Court on October 15, 1993, Justice JS Verma joined as the new Chief Justice and took his place on the bench. He pulled up the CBI for its casual attitude in the matter and decided to hold weekly meetings on the belatedly registered CBI case.

The CBI registered cases under the FERA as also under the Prevention of Corruption Act against the Jain brothers 'and others' and this led to arrest of Surendra Jain and his accountant, JK Jain on June 4, 1995 and both of them were remanded to jail. It was only after going to jail that Surendra Jain felt compelled to make his 'famous' 29-page statement to the CBI which implicated a number of senior Congress ministers and leaders of other political parties. Surendra Jain's statement also contained details of his payments to Narasimha Rao!

In the initial phase, the CBI raided the houses of some out-of-power politicians like Arif Mohammad Khan and Devi Lal and later submitted chargesheets against three Central ministers, viz., Balram Jakhar, SC Shukla and Madhav Rao Scindia; the list also included the names of BJP president LK Advani, former Union Ministers Arjun Singh and Yashwant Sinha, and Janata Dal leader Sharad Yadav. The list/chargesheets could not remain a secret, and 'the newspapers came out with screaming headlines, and the nation was scandalised'!

The three Central ministers resigned and LK Advani relinquished his seat in the Lok Sabha. Later Congress leaders like RK Dhawan, Kamal Nath and Bhajan Lal were also chargesheeted. Madan Lal Khurana (CM Delhi) had to quit on being implicated. Despite damaging evidence against him, Satish Sharma escaped as he was not a public servant during the relevant time.

Legal Framework for Combating Corruption

In the pre-independence period, the Indian Penal Code (IPC) was the main tool to combat corruption in public life. The Code had a chapter on 'Offences by Public Servants'. Sections 161 to 165 provided the legal framework to prosecute corrupt public servants.[11]

However, these IPC provisions as also the later Delhi Special Police Establishment Act (1946) were found to be utterly inadequate in the face of the ever-expanding spheres of corruption which gained considerable fillip in the wake of the Second World War, spawning not only newer forms of corruption but with much wider reach. This trend was further aggravated by newer forms of economic offences in the public as well as the private sectors much beyond the scope and the reach of not only the IPC but also the Prevention of Corruption Act of 1947. This legislation too was found to be inadequate in course of time and had to be amended or fresh legislation initiated. Thus, finally, the Prevention of Corruption Act of 1988 came into being, which is still the law on the subject of combating corruption.

However, in the wake of the process of economic liberalisation and consequent structural adjustment measures initiated by the Government of India in 1991 and continued thereafter by successive governments at the Centre and in the states, certain noticeable trends–some beneficial and some otherwise have been observed.

The rationale behind the adopted policy of liberalisation was four-fold: firstly, to foster a faster rate of economic growth; secondly, to provide a greater thrust for economic development, eventually leading to considerable reduction in the levels of poverty and unemployment. Thirdly, and importantly, these liberalisation measures were also expected to drastically reduce the levels of corruption not only in the governmental sectors but also in the corporate and financial sectors. Finally, the underlying hypothesis behind all such steps was, of course, the expectation that these measures and their consequent results would strengthen our democratic system and also lead to a healthier and more vibrant civil society.

To what extent the above objectives and societal expectations have been achieved or not is a debatable issue of multifaceted dimensions and as such, for our present purpose, we may not attempt here a conclusive dissertation touching on the rationale and also the modalities of economic liberalization. However, it needs to be admitted that our economic fabric has not undergone any glorious transformation as was touted initially or repeated periodically during the past two decades or more.

Growing menace of "Serious Economic Offences"

The remaining two issues, namely, the escalating levels of corruption in various segments of our governance and economy, especially the increasingly dangerous scale of black money generation through all conceivable, or not so conceivable, modus operandi of serious economic offences. What is more disturbing is the undeniable fact that neither our existing laws and regulations nor the enforcement agencies dealing with such crimes are capable of preventing, containing and controlling them substantially. Secondly, the inability of our prevailing system of criminal justice to punish the high-level economic offenders with the promptitude and severity expected by the society continues to be a cause for considerable anxiety.

Thus, "Nationalised Indian banks carry forty thousand crore rupees on their books as bad and doubtful debts, euphemistically called non-performing assets (NPAs)[12]". Such huge loot of public money goes on merrily, and silently, almost every year! No Finance Minister or the Governor of the Reserve Bank of India appear to have ever lost even a wink of sleep on this account. What a wonderful system we seem to have devised to ensure such huge loot year after year!

Another dark area is the *loot of public fund in respect of arms deals.* The global arms industry has emerged as one of the most important sources of corruption. According to the Stockholm International Peace Research Institute, arms trade is responsible for 40 per cent of all corruption in global transactions.... The high levels of concentration and secrecy in the arms industry and weapons trade greatly encourage the culture of corrupt practices... However, the cause of bigger concern is corruption dominating arms deals with developing and poor countries as this directly results in the denial of the basic needs of millions.

The damage goes much beyond money changing hands illegally, as in several cases, corruption leads to the sale of unnecessary military equipment or sale of much more expensive equipment even when cheaper alternatives are available.

"A country like India where millions of people can't meet their basic needs has emerged as the largest importer of weapons in the world..." (Bharat Dogra in *The Statesman* dated 14th July, 2012).

Inadequacy of existing laws, regulations and criminal justice system

Thus, almost since the 1990s, the citizens of India had the misfortune of being somewhat mute and helpless spectators to a disturbing spread of 'utter lawlessness' into banking, insurance, securities and other corporate and financial sectors. It is perhaps unquestionable that the ingenuity of the corrupt ones knows no bounds. The two successive massive stock market scams – the Harshad Mehta Security Scam and the subsequent Ketan Parekh Security Scam, both of the 1990s, amply demonstrated the 'innovativeness' of the scamsters and also how very ineffective our market regulatory authorities were.

The CPI MP Gurudas Das Gupta's well known 1993 publication '*A Report to the Nation on the (Harshad Mehta) Security Scam of 1992*' stated thus: "Today (1993) one knows that of the reported Rs 13,00,000 crore worth of securities transactions, the four foreign banks accounted for 56 per cent. Ten of their branches handled all the business, which landed the entire banking industry, including the foreign banks themselves, in such a mess". (p. 36). There is no need to think that the Indian banks were lagging behind. The Das Gupta Report continues:

"The joy of crossing the 4,000 mark by the BSE Sensex was, however, somewhat tempered by a news of a different sort. *The Times of India* and the *Economic Times* carried on 23rd April and 24th April 1992 sensational reports of a serious shortfall – Rs 600 crore – in the securities holdings of the country's premier nationalised bank, the State Bank of India. It transpired that the SBI was not only short of securities but had no record of their disappearance. The top management swung into instant action and their efforts seemed to bear fruit, when biggest of the bulls Harshad Mehta wrote out a cheque for Rs 380 crore and paid off the SBI. Over the next three days, three cheques aggregating Rs 220 crore were deposited and all dues of a grateful bank squared up". But this was not the end of the trouble for the banking industry. As the intrepid Das Gupta stated further:

"The key players in these events, which saw the overheating of the stock markets and the short sales of securities in the SBI, were not to know that the two seemingly unconnected events would haunt them for years to come. For, nobody at that time cared to investigate the magic source of Harshad Mehta's supplies. Not the SBI, certainly not the RBI. Nobody guessed the shortfall had been made up by breaking open the National Housing Bank.

"While the State Bank Managers were patting their backs for getting their own books in order and their own vaults refilled, another bank vault was being looted. This was the Reserve Bank of India's own subsidiary: The National Housing Bank.

"The mechanism of the fraud was simple. One broker had access to a number of bank funds. He only had to steal from one account to settle another. This went on till one day the chain snapped. A Pandora's Box was opened, revealing horrifying tales of frauds, forgeries, greed, back-stabbing and above all, treachery against the country and its 1.24 billion citizens.

"As the sordid tales came tumbling out, bank chiefs, public sector bosses, politicians, brokers and ministers were all found to be involved in the massive game of pulling out funds from development activities and channelising them into the stock markets, to keep financing an artificial boom, till the ordinary man was lured in with his honest savings to make the most of the bull run. When the flow of funds was checked, the market came crashing down like a house of cards. Alongside crashed the dreams of millions of small investors, some of them had lost their life's savings...". (Das Gupta Report, p. 17)[13]

Unprecedented Increase in Serious Economic Offences

Especially since the 1990s, we have witnessed a disturbing trend of serious financial frauds including tax evasion, black money generation, money laundering, benami and hawala transactions on the one hand and the spreading tentacles of heinous organised crimes like drugs and arms trafficking, narco-terrorism, etc. on the other.

On top of all such activities, the people have also been witnessing the growing but almost unchecked propensity on the part of the holders of high offices of trust and authority, both in the public and the private/corporate sectors in different parts of India to indulge in serious acts of malfeasance and gross misuse of public funds with impunity. In this context, the increasingly apparent evil nexus between politicians, public servants, business and industrial houses and the underworld is all too apparent. We may recall here the recent 2G Spectrum Scam running into perhaps several thousand crores of rupees and involving a cabinet minister of the

Government of India, still facing investigation and trial. We can continue wondering from our past experience of corruption by high profile holders of public office as to when trials of such cases will begin or end!

Our experience suggests that a tough law by itself does not guarantee its success in practice. In order to ensure that application of such stringent laws does not suffer from the known maladies of our criminal justice system as pointed out by the Malimath Committee on Criminal Justice Reforms, we may have to look for a new model of a tough law against serious economic offences along with new model of judicial forum built into the projected law. And that is what has been crafted by me while preparing the draft legislation titled "Serious Economic Offences (Prevention, Control, Investigation and Trial) Act".

Urgent need for a Serious Economic Offences Code

In addition to the above sordid saga of corruption and serious economic offences, the continuing revelations about the 2G Scam, the mining and allied scams in different states of India should call for a holistic approach towards corruption-cum-serious economic offences through a drastic forensic surgery coupled with determined executive operations of diverse kinds.

Anticipating the need for such a drastic and specially structured approach in respect of Serious Economic Offences, some faculty members and scholars of the West Bengal National University of Juridical Sciences (Kolkata) during 2003-04 painstakingly prepared, under my guidance as the then Adjunct Professor of the WB National University of Juridical Sciences (NUJS), a draft legislation titled 'Serious Economic Offences (Prevention, Control, Investigation And Trial) Act, 2004'. It was based on the expertise, mature judgement and collective wisdom of a very large body of concerned citizens of our country – law makers and law-enforcers, eminent jurists like Prof Madhava Menon and judges e.g., late AM Bhattacharjee, (former Chief Justice of the High Courts at Bombay and Calcutta), in addition to Justice VS Malimath and other judicial minds, financial, legal and other experts and concerned citizens from different parts of India.

On the other hand, the Government of India continues to provide thousands of crores of rupees of public funds to the states for various kinds of grandiose schemes such as Mahatma Gandhi National Rural Employment Guarantee Scheme (MNREGS), Sarvasiksha Abhiyan, national health schemes, etc. besides the scandalous MP Local Area Development (MPLAD) Scheme. Only a part of the above funds is utilised for the assigned purposes but the bulk of the money continues to be pilfered and openly looted by politicians and their henchmen in the states. And this is no secret, it is as much known to the concerned people in general as to the authorities in the Government of India and their counterparts in the states. This is nothing short of a national scandal of very serious proportion and the authorities concerned seem to be in the least bothered even in the face of such enormous wastage/pilferage of public funds. Hence, the need for much greater mobilisation of pressures from various quarters to ensure early enactment of an EOCI type of law and its strict application.

Salient features of the Serious Economic Offences Code For India (EOCI)

Definition of Serious Economic Offences: Serious Economic Offences for the purpose of this Code (EOCI) means and includes any offence involving dishonest, fraudulent or illegal transaction

- in respect of which the money or other property involved exceeds a value of Rs five crore or such other amount as may be prescribed in this behalf, and,
- includes (i) any suspected offence which appears to the competent/empowered Authority under this Code to involve serious or complex fraud, (ii) any such act or offence committed outside India which, had it taken place within India would have constituted an economic offence within the meaning of this Code.

Provided further that the offence or offences are such that these have or are reasonably suspected to have or likely to have "(i) grave social and/or national impact and implication for India's national economy and/or national security, or (ii) complex international ramifications/implications, (iii) a large number of Indian citizens as victims of such offences, and/or (iv) involvement of person or persons who are holders of high positions of public trust in government, public or private undertakings including banks, other financial institutions, regulatory or corporate bodies, statutory or otherwise".

2. Other features of the proposed Act/EOCI:

- The proposed Code should be a federal one with all-India jurisdiction. Appropriate Constitutional and other related amendments in statutes may have to be made in consultation with the Chief Ministers of states, with a categorical assurance and supporting statutory mechanisms to ensure that such a Code shall not and cannot be misused for political, partisan and other extraneous considerations.

- To ensure the above, there should be a Competent Authority under the Code which must be a high-powered and autonomous one, to effectively "administer, enforce and implement the EOCI - only 'in the interest of the country' and it must be free from executive fiat and extraneous pressures and having all-India jurisdiction. It should be a statutory body like the National Human Rights Commission (NHRC) but unlike the NHRC, the proposed Authority should not be an advisory or recommendatory body only.

- The aforesaid Authority may be chaired by a former Judge of the Supreme Court or a former Chief Justice of a High Court, and having four or five other members, all of whom must be of high personal integrity with known credibility, expertise and knowledge in intelligence gathering, functioning of banks and other financial sectors, investigation into serious economic offences and legal matters including prosecution.

- To ensure effective functioning of the aforesaid authority, it should have four distinct divisions under it: (1) Intelligence (collection, collation and analysis) Division; (2) Inquiry and Investigation Division; (3) Legal Advice and Prosecution Division, and (4) Administrative and Logistics Division.

- Special provisions have also been made in the EOCI[14] for an innovative judicial forum for dealing with serious economic offences as also special rules of procedure, evidence and trial of such cases coming within the purview of the EOCI".

Onset of a 'dark age' in India ?

For far too long, we Indians have been indulging in self-glorification by asserting that we are the inheritors of a 'great civilisation', that 'Mera Bharat Mahan', that spiritualism as opposed to materialism, is in our blood and so on and so forth. Perhaps for brief spells in our recorded history, we were endowed with some of the above noble qualities, especially for a brief spell of nearly sixty years, from the last decade of the 19th century till about the middle of the twentieth.

It is noteworthy that during this period some of the great sons of our soil were born who were untiring in their efforts at bringing out the best in us as human beings - in the fields of social reform, religion, culture, education coupled with an untiring yearning for freedom from foreign rule, emancipation of women and the downtrodden and so on. Raja Ram Mohan Roy, Pandit Ishwar Chandra Vidyasagar, Rabindranath Tagore, Swami Vivekananda, Dayanand Saraswati, Sir Asutosh Mukherjee and his son Shyama Prosad Mukherjee, Lala Lajpat Rai, Balgangadhar Tilak, Mohandas Karamchand Gandhi, Subhas Chandra Bose and many other equally notable personalities and great sons of India were born in different parts of the country during the above period. Surprisingly enough, virtually all of them and many more were products of this brief period of our history.

A 'dark age' since the '60s of the 20th Century ?

A 'dark age' seems to have overtaken us since the sixties of the 20th century, especially marked in the spheres of our moral and ethical values, in education, governance and administration. This decay and degeneration have been most damagingly manifest in the functioning of the political parties, especially in the spheres of electoral politics. According to many concerned citizens, the understanding and acceptance of this stark reality of the past and the present, should be the first lesson which we have to accept for the success of any serious endeavour of national awareness-building against corruption, if we sincerely intend to lay the foundation for a healthier nation-building and social regeneration.

The cumulative manifestation of the resultant ills of the past and the present is the unquestionable spectre of widespread corruption affecting virtually all spheres of our national life. Historians and sociologists alike would agree that the corrosive effects of corruption have generally been the precursor of a nation's decay. A disturbing thought indeed for all concerned citizens of this country. But it is a lesson of history which we persistently ignore and refuse to seriously come to grips with.

And what is worse, those at the apex of our national life and various fields of activity are themselves either the guilty persons or are devoid of unquestioned credibility and sense of responsibility. Hence, any hope and expectation that such leaders at national and state levels would somehow and some day be able to eradicate, or even drastically curb the prevailing cesspool of corruption and decay would be totally misplaced. Such a Buddha-like miracle towards 'nirvana' (emancipation) is most unlikely to happen. This is the second lesson, I believe, for any serious crusade against corruption. Again, a very sobering thought indeed!

And a hard look around us will amply testify to this phenomenon.

- The Supreme Court order of July, 2001 asked Chandrashekhar (a former Prime Minister of India!) to surrender 500 acres of forest land in his possession around his Bhondsi *ashram* near Gurgaon in Haryana which was alleged to have been illegally acquired by him. (*The Statesman* dt. 20.04.2002 and 22.04.2002).
- In yet another order in April 2002, the Supreme Court directed Chandrashekhar's *Bharat Yatra Trust* to hand over to Haryana Government within two months a 51-acre plot of land around the above *ashram* on the outskirts of Delhi. The apex court also imposed a cost/penalty of Rs 25,000/ on the Trust for illegally occupying the village land, and further directing the Haryana Government to take back the land. (*Hindustan Times* dt. 22.04.2002). Could there be a more humiliating treat for a former MP and a Prime Minister of our country!
- Another very disturbing disclosure was about the unimaginable type and magnitude of corruption on the part of the holder of an honourable (?) constitutional office. We are referring to the *modus operandi* and wide network of corruption allegedly perpetrated by the then Chairman of the Punjab Public Service Commission, namely, Ravinderpal Singh Sidhu (*Hindustan Times* dt. 21.04.2002 and 25.04.2002).

- A similar exposure later related to the allegedly corrupt practices of the Chairman of Maharashtra Public Service Commission, which badly tarnished the credibility of such bastions of probity and fair play.
- We must not fail to mention at this stage the staggering levels of corruption in the matter of the 2G Spectrum licence distribution and the Commonwealth Games scams involving several thousand crores of public money and indulged in by holders of high public offices. Thanks to our painfully slow criminal justice system, one wonders whether the guilty persons will be adequately and in a deterrent manner punished during their life time.

Like many other self-respecting citizens of India, I too am humbled by the Transparency International's 'Corruption Perception Index/2000' under which India ranks at 69 out of 90 countries. There may be scope for serious debate about the nuances of the yardsticks followed by the TI in arriving at the above gradings. Even presuming that some day and by some modified criteria, India ranks at 51 in terms of the corruption perception index (very unlikely in the foreseeable future !) should we not still be ashamed as Indian citizens that we fail to belong to the top 5-10 countries perceived to be the least corrupt ?

In our thinking, therefore, the third lesson should be to inculcate in us the basic honesty to admit that we should learn to feel genuinely ashamed, individually and collectively, when we have done or are about to indulge in or be party, directly or indirectly, to something amounting to dishonesty. And this could be the first step towards cleansing ourselves individually and collectively from the disgraceful grip and spectacle of corruption.

Is India a corrupt country?

In spite of what has been stated above, I do not agree that "India is a corrupt country[15]". There are good reasons to hold that a large majority of our people, in all walks of life and in all socio economic strata are not corrupt – some due to their moral, ethical, spiritual or religious convictions, some by virtue of their immediate family or hereditary conditioning and, of course, there would be some who did not get the 'opportunity' of indulging in corrupt practices!

The *fourth lesson,* therefore, would be to devise methods whereby the aforesaid inhibiting factors – moral, spiritual, religious, family and other inhibiting factors against corruption – are nourished and strengthened. Hopefully, this in turn, would generate ideas and help in building up a carefully crafted short-term and long-term strategy to substantially lessen the grip of corruption and lead to eventual bulwark of expected urge and also the mass upsurge for a largely corruption-free society.

It would be short-sighted to depend only, or even largely, on government-led anti-corruption measures. This, however, must not be misinterpreted that the governments, both at central and state levels, will have no role to play in this anti-corruption strategy. On the other hand, the central and state governments and their respective agencies must play a critical role, somewhat like a catalytic agent – encouraging, assisting, motivating and even providing finances in certain instances so that many NGOs and other socially committed individuals and institutions can play a more meaningful and active anti-corruption oriented roles in various parts of our country.

In the above context, we may take note of the recent anti-corruption agitation led by social activist Anna Hazare and his associates. This agitation, according to some people, created considerable awakening among a large cross-section of the people in various parts of India. But this got dissipated in the wake of the short-sighted controversy generated by the Anna Hazare group led confrontation with the Central Government over their Jan Lokpal draft as against the Lokpal Bill of the government. And what has been the net outcome?

Most people, otherwise genuinely interested in an effective anti-corruption mechanism, lost their patience as well as faith in the efficacy of both modules, leaving behind a noxious trail of charges against some of the Hazare team members and, of course, counter-charges by the Hazare team members against the people in power. The net result of the above unfortunate, but predictable, course of events is that we, the concerned people, stand where we were, leaving the core issues, namely, corruption and measures to check the same unresolved!

In a fairly recent interview, the CPM supremo Prakash Karat[16] blamed the recent spate of corruption due to the economic liberalisation policy of the Government of India and his prescription for this malady was to "strike at the nexus of big business, politicians and bureaucrats". (Frontline, September 23, 2011, pp. 26-27).

The malady is much too deep-rooted and its eradication will call for multi faceted remedies. And even then, it needs to be admitted that no country in the world, not even the erstwhile Communist regime in the Soviet

Union or the current regime in China or for that matter most of the countries in Europe, South (Latin) America, to name a few, are free from the malady of widespread corruption and that too in high places of governance.

So, what is the way out of this malaise? How do we curb corruption in a vast country like India, with extremes of poverty and affluence, with widespread illiteracy and fairly weak enforcement machineries, a dilatory, ambivalent and costly judicial system?

Keeping the above constraints in view, I would take the liberty of sharing with my readers a few of my observations, mostly not theoretical, after having worked for nearly 14-15 years in the Government of India in the country's premier anti-corruption investigation agency, namely, the Central Bureau of Investigation (CBI) as the DIG of Delhi Metropolitan Branch (1974-77), then known as the largest of the CBI branches, dealing with both anti-corruption wing as also its economic offences wing.

This was followed by my exposure to the largely unknown CBI's Special Unit (SU), under the direct supervision of the Director, CBI as it dealt with CBI Intelligence about highly-placed officers of the Central Government/Central PSUs including their nexus with 'undesirable contacts', usually in business or otherwise. The SU also used to keep a tab on the conduct of the CBI officers; and based on its reports, after meticulous check/verification/investigation, a few CBI officers of various ranks were either quietly 'eased out', or suspended or even chargesheeted in criminal cases for their trial in appropriate courts of law. This was a desirable, healthy and necessary check on any kind of misconduct or even misdemeanour of CBI officers of all ranks.

The CBI had, and perhaps still has a number of specialised investigation branches in its HQ in Delhi as also in its various branches located in most states. But it would be naïve to hold that the widespread malaise of corruption could be eradicated by the CBI itself despite its branches in all the states. CBI does have a deterrence in all departments of the Government of India but it would be presumptuous to think that the CBI is the only answer to the pervasive atmosphere of corruption, not confined to government departments only.

One look at the corruption scenario in our country – in and outside the government departments, corruption in politics, in the very stream of electoral politics, functioning of the numerous political parties, some with known notoriety and bulging money bags in innumerable numbers, fake/false bank accounts in India and abroad and it would be a futile exercise to identify them. A costly electoral politics itself gives rise to myriads of electoral and related malpractices which defies a simplistic description or cataloguing. And yet all efforts at a drastic electoral reform has largely proved futile, despite the efforts of successive Election Commissions and many others in the civil society. The recent controversy about the Lokpal Bill and Jan Lokpal Bill proved equally unproductive for various reasons.

West Bengal Vigilance Commission

After my retirement from service, I was inducted by West Bengal Government in 1993 to the highest anti-corruption agency in the state, namely, the Vigilance Commission as its head. Till then the Vigilance Commission in West Bengal used to be headed by a retired chief justice or retired judge of the Calcutta High Court or by retired chief secretaries of the state. I learnt that the Vigilance Commission was considered by most people in or outside government as a non-functional entity for nearly two decades, and this state of affairs suited the ministers and the heads of different departments of the government. Hence, my taking over as the Vigilance Commissioner was obviously viewed with some alarm, at least by a certain section of the bureaucracy as was evident from the following: unknown to me, Chief Minister, Jyoti Basu had asked the Home Department as also the Chief Secretary to issue my appointment letter at an early date to ensure that I could assume charge as the Vigilance Commissioner within the next 10-15 days.

Jyoti Basu, being a shrewd judge of bureaucratic conduct, asked his Special Assistant Joy Krishna Ghosh after about three weeks to find out the date on which I had taken over charge as the State's Vigilance Commissioner. When Ghosh rang me up at my residence, I told him that no order to that effect had reached me till then. I learnt later that the Chief Minister, thereafter expressed his strong annoyance to the Chief Secretary for his instruction in this regard not having been followed up even after 2-3 weeks; he further ordered the Chief Secretary to ensure that the government order appointing me as the State's Vigilance Commissioner was issued forthwith and that the same was to be delivered at my Salt Lake residence by a special messenger the same evening!

The above development was orally conveyed to me by the CM's Special Assistant who also stated that, as desired by the CM, I should join as the Vigilance Commissioner the next day or as soon thereafter as possible on receiving the government order about my new assignment.

After joining the Vigilance Commission, I started getting myself acquainted with the details of its functioning, its strengths and weaknesses, possible remedial measures which could be initiated within the Commission or through the government. For this, I held a series of meetings with the Commission staff at various levels.

The Vigilance Commission has three wings:

(a) *Anti-Corruption Branch* (ACB), largely manned by police officers of various ranks (IGP/DIG/SPs/Dy SPs/Inspectors/Sub-Inspectors/Assistant Sub-Inspectors and some supporting subordinate staff)

(b) *Administrative Branch* headed by an officer of the rank of a Secretary in the State Government + one officer of the rank of a Deputy Secretary/two Assistant Secretaries and some other supporting staff as Upper Division Assistants and Lower Division Assistants, besides a few Stenographers, one exclusively for the VC.

(c) The third is known as the Legal Branch with only one Law Officer, but a very competent person with legal background.

(d) The fourth was known as the *Commissioners of Departmental Enquiries* (CDEs), mostly with legal background or past experience in dealing with departmental inquiry proceedings.

(e) The fifth one was known as the *Technical Division*, with two or three officers with civil/electrical/mechanical/ engineering or auditing background.

I learnt to my dismay that the Commission being only a recommendatory body, could send its detailed inquiry reports to the heads of the concerned government departments through the Chief Secretary for necessary follow-up actions. In most cases, the Commission's reports/recommendations used to be routinely forwarded by the Chief Secretary. No feedback was called for or received by the Chief Secretary, and the Commission was not favoured with any feedback either from the Chief Secretary or from the departments concerned. After a couple of months, I discussed this unfortunate state of affairs with the Chief Minister, who expressed his unhappiness at this and then wanted to know what remedial measure could be taken. I stated that I would like to brief him about the results (i.e., action taken/not taken) by the heads of departments every three months, for which a meeting should be held in his room in which the Chief Secretary should also be present besides myself. And this was readily endorsed by the Chief Minister.

So, the message went round that the departmental heads as also the Chief Secretary will be required to act on the Commission's recommendations and that the results of action taken/not taken (with reasons for the same) will have to be communicated to the Vigilance Commissioner for being brought to the notice of the Chief Minister every three months. Some progress, to start with, resulting in some jitters in the corridors of the Writers' Buildings. I could make out that the departmental heads, by and large, sat up and started paying some attention to reports emanating from the Vigilance Commission and we started receiving at least some feedback from the departments on the reports/recommendations of the Commission.

In view of my CBI background, it was possible to initiate some fresh measures, though many not to the liking of some bureaucrats. But, by and large, I started receiving positive and encouraging feedbacks from many of the secretaries and other departmental heads. I was in the Vigilance Commission for about three years, but I must admit that in the prevailing milieu, one could not expect to produce any earth-shaking changes in the functioning of the various departments of the state government. However, on the eve of my departure from the above Commission, I prepared a detailed note, incorporating my suggestions for further improvement in its functioning. But I doubt if any serious or sustained attention to the suggestions in my note has been paid as yet.

Where do we begin the Anti-Corruption Movement?

School-going children to be the starting point: A valuable experiment in Australia

The crucial question to be answered at this stage is: where do we begin this gigantic endeavour of awareness-building against corruption and how do we go about this task? My humble submission is: let us begin at the beginning – with the school children, especially when they are in the age-group of 6 to 16 years. In this respect we may adopt, and suitably adapt the models practised in some of the low-corruption countries.

In Australia, for instance, perhaps two or three decade ago, their Independent Commission Against Corruption (ICAC) developed imaginative audio-visual aids like CD-ROMs for various levels of students (mainly school students) for use not only in classes but for their homes as well. This was part of their Science and Technology syllabus to motivate students to learn about their 'natural' flora, fauna, rivers and rivulets, streams, etc. and 'man-made' environments including aspects of violence, corruption, various noticeable malpractices like crime and other noticeable anti-social behaviour in society and as also in their known family environments. These were woven around an imaginary village and its inhabitants so as to give it a semblance of real-life situations in which the students were motivated/encouraged even to point out any deviance on the part of their elders.

What is of significance for our purpose is that key ethical considerations and value certification were interwoven throughout the syllabi and the CD-ROMs, without trying to sermonize, which we usually try to do all the time and from all questionable quarters, by harping on what some of our revered saints and saintly persons had taught us in the hoary past. We have observed over the decades that this archaic practice is least likely to touch the hearts and minds, especially of the younger and school-going generation.

This generation especially should be allowed to think for themselves, which the Australian model substantially succeeded in achieving through their novel methodology. Even 5-10 years old boys and girls developed an instinctive antipathy towards destruction of plants and animals, drug–addiction and smoking, child abuse and other forms of violence; they also could imbibe from such impressionable age that corrupt practices in many forms were not only morally and ethically harmful and as such needed to be resisted through individual, family and group efforts. Many examples of these were built into the syllabi and also powerfully projected through the CD-ROMS. These were widely circulated and projected through various media in Australia under the aegis of the ICAC and titled *The Talk of TOPPSVILLE* and during those years were available from the ICAC approved GM Interactive Pty Ltd., 166 Willoughby Road, Crows Nest, New South Wales-2065 (Australia).[17]

Therefore, the fifth and the most crucial lesson for anti-corruption awareness building is to begin the process with the children of the school-going age. However, we should not fail to take note of the Indian reality - in which many boys and girls of tender age, mostly living in the midst of poverty and malnutrition, are outside the realm of our formal educational system. Hence, we have to devise special measures to reach out to this segment of our younger generation with innovative efforts and in some modified format which may be relevant to their life and living conditions.

Who should be the change agents ?

Finally, who do we visualise as the change agents for such a crucial and gigantic task of immense and lasting value for our entire community? Let us make at least a tentative effort to list them out briefly:

- *School teachers* obviously would be expected to play the crucial role at the most formative stage in the life of our children. This, obviously, will be in addition to the expected role of their *parents* at home. *Writers of school text books* will also be expected to play a constructive role, keeping in view the important inputs towards eventual moulding of the minds of the school students.
- *Cinema, theatre and TV script writers, producers and directors* as also some of *their sponsors* should be motivated to devote at least some part of their creative activities on the above lines, including the

Australian *TOPPSVILLE* model or something even better suited to our socio economic conditions.

- In addition to the above, the print and electronic media may also be two of the most potent channels of communication and transmission of the above themes for our school children and other members of our young generation - the common theme and objective being to motivate them against the pervasive corrupt practices in various walks of our social and national life and also to foster in them an abiding respect for treading the path of rectitude in their present and future life. They may simultaneously be enthused to motivate others in following these values and practices.
- *Some of our socially motivated citizens and NGOs* would undoubtedly be expected to play an important and catalytic role on the above themes and objectives.
- We should not ignore the value of some other unorganised but socially active institutions like our *folk singers and folk artists* spread all over the country and cutting across caste, communal and linguistic barriers. These traditional and age-old social institutions may also be suitably motivated and mobilised to play their valuable part on the above themes and objectives.
- The million-dollar question to be answered now is: who should play the *crucial* and *catalytic role* in both *motivating and suitably mobilising* the aforesaid and many other un-named individuals, groups and associations? There is just no simple answer to the above. This task will have to be voluntarily performed by us all, individually as well as collectively, if we desire to be known as the worthy citizens of our country called INDIA.

References

1 *The Pathology of Corruption* by SS Gill, HarperCollins, New Delhi, 1998, p. 33.

2 Gill, op. cit., pp. 33-36.

3 Op. cit., p. 56.

4 SS Gill, *The Pathology of Corruption*, HarperCollins, India, New Delhi, 1999, p. 62.

5 Gill, op. cit., p. 63.

6 Gill, op. cit., p. 64.

7 Gill, op. cit., p. 79.

8 Gill, op. cit., p. 80.

9 Gill, op.cit., p. 81.

10 Gill, op. cit., p. 97.

11 Chapter 3 of the *Fourth Report of the Second Administrative Reforms Commission (of India)* titled "Ethics in Governance", p. 58, January 2007.

12 Gill, op. cit., p. 158.

13 Das Gupta was also a prominent member of the Joint Parliamentary Committee on the Harshad Mehta Securities Scam, which the Government and the Parliament were forced to constitute to go into the details of the scam and to make suitable recommendations.

14 For further details, may refer to the NUJS paper titled "Serious Economic Offences Code" (EOCI)/ 2004.

15 The above statement was made by N Vittal, former Central Vigilance Commissioner, in his talk delivered at the SVP National Police Academy, Hyderabad on 6th June, 2001 and as reproduced in the journal *Vigilance Professional*, vol 4, dated 4 July, 2001.

16 Did they, viz., Karat and his party succeed in eradicating the well-known above nexus even in the two states (Kerala and West Bengal) ruled by them for a considerable period of time? The answer, obviously, is in the negative, for the simple reason that, howsoever tempting, theoretical posturings will not succeed.

17 This was the position in 1977-80 and I am not quite sure if it still persists.

Index

Books of Related Interest

Conspiracy to kill Rajiv Gandhi
From CBI Files

K Ragothaman
Former SP - CBI

ISBN: 978-81-7049-450-8
Rs. 595.00 $ 35.00

Voice of CBI

M Narayanan
(Ex-Jt Director, CBI)

ISBN: 978-81-7049-467-6
Rs. 595.00 $ 35.00

CBI Top Cop Recalls

SK Datta, IPS
Former Director, CBI

ISBN: 978-81-7049-320-4
Rs. 695.00 $ 40.00

Inside IB and RAW
The Rolling Stone That Gathered Moss

K Sankaran Nair
Former Head Research and Analysis Wing (RAW) (India's External Intelligence Agency) & Indian High Commissioner: Singapore

ISBN: 978-81-7049-305-1
Rs. 495.00 $ 30.00

Who Owns CBI:
The Naked Truth

BR Lall, IPS
(Former Joint Director, Central Bureau of Investigation (CBI) and Director General of Police, Haryana)

ISBN: 81-7049-293-9
Rs. 495.00 $ 30.00

Intelligence Tradecraft
Secrets of Spy Warfare

MK Dhar, IPS
Former: Jt. Dir, IB

ISBN: 978-81-7049-399-0
Rs. 795.00 $ 45.00

Operation Triple X:
An Indian Spy-Run in Pakistan

A Novel by
Maloy Krishna Dhar, IPS
(Former Jt. Chief of IB)

ISBN: 81-7049-301-3
Rs. 495.00 $ 30.00

Fulcrum of Evil:
ISI-CIA-Al Qaeda Nexus

Maloy Krishna Dhar, IPS
(Former Joint Director,
Intelligence Bureau, India)

ISBN: 81-7049-278-5
Rs. 795.00 $ 45.00

Pakistan's Intelligence

Sudhakar Raje
Former Indian Diplomat

ISBN: 978-81-7049-382-2
Rs. 795.00 $ 45.00

Intelligence For Management

DC Pathak, IPS

ISBN: 81-7049-377-8
Rs. 495.00 $ 30.00

Manual of Intelligence Operations

US Marine Corps

ISBN: 978-81-7049-388-4
Rs. 595.00 US $ 35.00

Intelligence, Security & Asymmetric Warfare

Dhirendra Singh, IAS
Lt Gen **DB Shekatkar**

ISBN: 978-81-7049-379-2
Rs. 595.00 US $ 35.00

Why Secret Intelligence Fails

Michael A. Turner

ISBN: 81-7049-292-0
Rs. 695.00 $ 35.00

Effective Interrogation
Naxalism - Police - Intelligence

G Chatterjee
Former: Intelligence Officer, India

ISBN: 978-81-7049-375-4
Rs. 595.00 $ 35.00

Reforming Intelligence Agencies:
Pakistan's Transitional Democracy

Frédéric Grare

ISBN: 978-81-7049-398-3
Rs. 595.00 US $ 35.00

The ISI Game Plan

A Novel by
YPS Mohan

ISBN: 978-81-7049-356-3
Rs. 495.00 $ 30.00

Intelligence:
A Security Weapon

D.C. Pathak, IPS
(Former Chief of Intelligence Bureau, India)

ISBN: 81-7049-166-5
Rs. 595.00 $ 35.00

Strategies in Defence and Intelligence

Lt. Gen. S. Pattabhiraman
M.K.Dhar, IPS etc.

ISBN: 978-81-7049-336-5
Rs. 495.00 $ 30.00

India's External Intelligence:
Secrets of Research and Analysis Wing (RAW)

Major General VK Singh

ISBN: 81-7049-332-3
Rs. 495.00 $ 30.00

India's Spy Agencies:
Shaken not Stirred

Lt Col Sunil S Parihar

ISBN: 978-81-7049-438-6
Rs. 595.00 $ 35.00

CBI Headquarters:
Victory or Mystery?

D Mukherjee, IPS

ISBN: 978-81-7049-447-8
Rs. 595.00 $ 35.00

Open Secrets:
India's Intelligence Unveiled

M.K. Dhar, IPS
(Former Joint Chief of India's Intelligence Bureau)

ISBN: 81-7049-216-5 (HB)
Rs. 795.00
ISBN: 81-7049-240-8 (PB)
Rs. 495.00 $ 45.00

Free the CBI:
Power Games in Bhopal & other Cases

BR Lall, IPS
Former: Joint Director-CBI
DGP Haryana

ISBN: 978-81-7049-396-9
Rs. 495.00 $ 35.00

Intelligence:
Corporate Success and Vigilance

DC Pathak, IPS
Member: National Security Advisory Board and Former Director, Intelligence Bureau, India

ISBN: 81-7049-289-0
Rs. 495.00 $ 30.00